THE GOSPEL OF YESHUA

THE GOSPEL

OF

YESHUA

A Fresh Look at the Life and Teaching of Jesus

SKIP JOHNSON

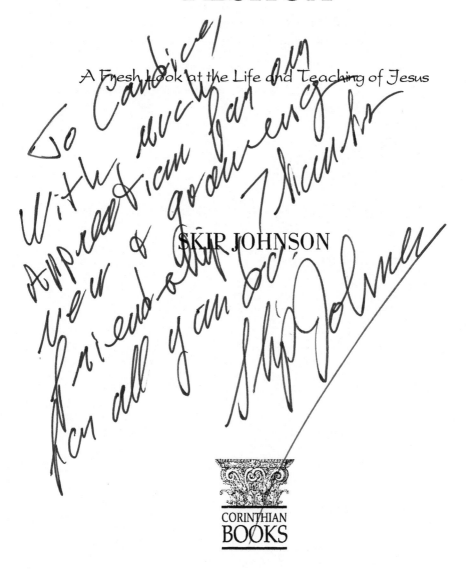

CORINTHIAN
BOOKS

Mount Pleasant, S.C.

Publisher's Cataloguing-in-Publication
(Provided by Quality Books, Inc.):

Johnson, Skip.
  The Gospel of Yeshua: a fresh look at the life and teaching of
Jesus / by Skip Johnson. — 1st ed.
    p. cm.
    LCCN: 00-107982
    ISBN 1-929175-03-5 (hc)
    ISBN 1-929175-24-8 (sc)

  1. Jesus Christ—Biography—Fiction. 2. Jesus Christ—Teachings—Fiction.   I. Title.

PS3560.O386425Go 2001   813.'6
                                          QBI00-795

Corinthian Books
an imprint of The Côté Literary Group
P.O. Box 1898
Mt. Pleasant, S.C. 29465-1898
(843) 881-6080
http://www.corinthianbooks.com

Preface

Anyone who tries to write the story of Jesus learns very quickly why it cannot be done. Regardless of what some churches insist, it is impossible because there is no single story of Jesus.

The four primary sources of information about him — the books of Matthew, Mark, Luke, and John — often contradict one another. John differs so radically from the other three that it often appears they were not even writing about the same person.

John shows Jesus declaring his Messiahship at the beginning of his ministry, repeating the claim so often it almost becomes a mantra. Matthew, Mark, and Luke all show Jesus going to great lengths throughout his ministry to specifically avoid being identified as the Messiah. (Matthew and Luke never quote Jesus as claiming to be the Messiah, and although Mark quotes him one time as claiming the title [Mark 14:62], that claim came very late in his life, was made under very dubious circumstances, and was never repeated despite several opportunities to do so.)

Also, John says Jesus' career lasted three years and he cleansed the temple at the beginning of it. Matthew, Mark, and Luke (who together are called the "synoptic Gospels" because they agree on most major points) say Jesus' career lasted one year and he cleansed the temple at the end of it.

Furthermore, John says Jesus performed the astonishing feat of bringing a dead man (Lazarus) back to life. None of the synoptic Gospels mentions that feat, although it seems that if they had known about it, they certainly would have written about it.

John and the synoptic Gospels contradict each other even on matters of emphasis and style. The synoptic Gospels place extreme importance on Jesus' baptism, temptations, transfiguration, and the events in the Garden of Gethsemane. John doesn't mention any of them.

The synoptic Gospels depict Jesus as using parables and short proverbs as his primary teaching tools, and they never show him speaking in long allegories. John depicts Jesus as often speaking in long and complicated allegories, but never using parables and rarely using short proverbs.

Biblical scholars usually explain the fundamental discrepancies between the accounts by saying the synoptic Gospels were written to tell the factual story of Jesus, and John was written as a spiritual book to explain the story — much like the difference between a newspaper's news and editorial pages.

But even if John is eliminated as a source, the synoptic Gospels still cannot be relied on to tell 'the' story of Jesus, because even they contradict one another on many important details. They differ as to who attended Jesus' birth and what happened there, who saw and heard what at his baptism, who attended his crucifixion, what words he spoke from the cross, and exactly what happened on that all-important Sunday morning after he died.

Another problem that makes telling 'the' story of Jesus impossible is that the information we have is spotty and woefully incomplete. Aside from the conflicting accounts of his birth, and a single vignette about him when he was about thirteen, the Gospels tell us nothing about Jesus until he begins his ministry at about age thirty. Even after the ministry begins, the Gospels' accounts, in addition to contradicting one another, often raise questions they do not answer.

Yet another problem with writing the story of Jesus is that we are not privy to the thinking processes of anyone involved, and so we do not know what motivated them. Just one of many examples:

Why did Judas betray Jesus? For the money (about twenty dollars by today's standards)? Out of hatred? To force Jesus to move against Rome? Because of jealousy? Fear? Blackmail? No one knows for certain.

However, just because there is no one story of Jesus, it does not mean an accurate accounting of his life cannot be made. The synoptic Gospels relate enough harmonizing information about Jesus, especially after he begins his ministry, to provide a strong framework for a narrative. Plus, modern scholarship has uncovered vast amounts of knowledge in recent years that can be read back into the known facts to flesh out the story.

For instance, we know from the Gospel accounts that Jesus grew up in Nazareth two thousand years ago. The accounts reveal nothing about his life during those years, but modern research tells us what life would have been like for any boy who grew up in Nazareth at that time, allowing us to read back into Jesus' life the economic, religious, social, and political situations that would have influenced him. We know how his house would have been designed and constructed, what his home life would have been like, how he would have been educated in secular matters, what his religious training would have been, what special opportunities for travel and learning he would have had by virtue of where he lived. The picture of his childhood that emerges is clear and well documented.

Research also has provided many answers to questions that are not apparent from reading the Gospels. Why, for example, did Jesus appear to work many miracles throughout his life after he specifically rejected the temptation to do so? Why was his trial before the temple rulers illegal? Why did Pontius Pilate, Rome's procurator (governor) of Palestine, have Jesus crucified when he knew Jesus was innocent of every charge against him?

Putting the Gospels' accounts together with the results of modern research provides plenty of information to write an accurate, although of necessity a fictionalized, narrative of Jesus' life. However, because the historical Jesus must differ from any fictionalized Jesus, I have elected to honor that difference, and avoid confusion, by replacing the name Jesus with Yeshua. Yeshua is actually closer to the name Jesus' contemporaries would have known him by.

But — and this is crucial — the differences between Jesus and Yeshua are entirely superficial, and they always relate only to the physical details of Jesus' life, never to his teaching. Matthew, Mark, and Luke speak with a single, clear, strong voice about his teaching. Even John, despite telling such a drastically different story from the one told by the synoptic Gospels, concurs with them absolutely about Jesus' teaching on love.

So, I repeat for the sake of emphasis: Although interpretations of the biblical accounts will vary — Christians may never agree about the miracle stories, for instance, or why Judas betrayed Jesus — the teaching of Yeshua in this book is precisely the teaching of Jesus, as Jesus' disciples would have understood it.

Generally, I have followed the rules of journalism wherever possible in writing this narrative. Whenever fact is known, either from ancient writings or modern research, I write fact.

Whenever fact is not known, I fill in the spaces — I connect the dots, as it were — with what all biblical scholars agree could have happened, and many say probably did happen.

Because no book can be any better than its sources, the reader should know my sources. They are many, but particularly helpful to me early on were the seventeen-volume *The Daily Bible Study Series* by William Barclay, and *The Life and Teaching of Jesus* by Edward W. Bauman, both published by Westminster Press.

Readers familiar with either writer's timeless work will notice their fingerprints throughout this book.

Other sources that were important to me (in addition to several versions of Matthew, Mark, Luke, and John) included *The Interpreter's Bible,* published by Abingdon; *The Bible Almanac,* edited by J.I. Packer, Merrill C. Tenney, and William White Jr., published by Thomas Nelson Publishers; *Herod: King of the Jews and Friend of the Romans,* by Peter Richardson, published by the University of South Carolina Press; *Essential Judaism,* by George Robinson, published by Pocket Books; and *Jesus of Nazareth, King of the Jews,* by Paula Fredriksen, published by Alfred A. Knopf.

I used many other written sources as well, but my single most important source has been my own experience.

It was 1977. I was thirty-eight, married, and the father of two daughters. I had just lost my job and saw no immediate prospects for getting another one. My personal life had been filled with late-night partying and heavy drinking. I was beginning to feel distraught and depressed.

Probably because I had been reared in churches, and although it had been many years since I had taken churches or religion seriously, I started thinking about Jesus. The more I thought, the more I realized how very little I really knew about him.

Like most people who have attended church with any regularity, I was familiar with various stories about Jesus. I could quote his parables and I knew all the miracle stories, but when I thought about it, I realized I could not put them together to form a complete whole. I could not narrate his life.

I certainly could not say what he had done that, as an anonymous poet wrote, affected humankind more than "all the armies that ever marched, all the navies that ever sailed, all the parliaments that ever sat, all the kings that ever reigned, put together." It was sobering to realize I knew more about some current sports figures and other passing celebrities than I did about that man.

I started reading about Jesus, and the more I learned, the more he intrigued me. It occurred to me that if his teaching was true, then I or anyone else could prove it. All I would have to do is live his teaching. If I did, I would either consistently realize his promises, in which case his teaching must be true, or I would not consistently realize his promises, in which case Jesus must have been either a liar or a madman—or both.

Over the next several years, I experimented with his teaching, and learned that whenever I was able to put his teaching into effect, it worked. That experience, which was repeated consistently, helped keep me searching for the deeper story of Jesus, and what I kept finding constantly amazed me.

There was so much I did not know, and even more I thought I knew, but did not. I constantly asked myself why didn't I know this? Why didn't everyone know this?

I took voluminous notes on my personal research, a habit formed by thirty years as a journalist, and eventually used those notes to write and teach a twelve-session study course for adults on the life and teaching of Jesus. I presented the course to several groups that included people from a wide variety of religious backgrounds — liberal and conservative Protestants, Roman Catholics, Jews, agnostics, and many others. The course was received so enthusiastically that I decided to use it as the basis for a narrative about the life and teaching of Jesus.

But I did not have enough information. I knew facts of Jesus' life, but I did not feel his surroundings. I needed to walk where he walked, pause where he paused, visit where he visited, see what he saw — saturate myself, as much as possible, in whatever atmosphere still survived from his day. With that in mind, my wife, Sue, and I traveled to the Holy Land to trace as much as possible the steps Jesus took two thousand years ago.

Sometimes it was impossible. In Jerusalem, only a part of one wall remains from the awesome, wonder-of-the-world temple that Jesus knew. Furthermore, virtually every patch of land in and around Jerusalem that Jesus is thought to have visited has been buried under cathedrals, shrines, mosques, monasteries, and other religious structures, making it impossible to see much of the landscape as Jesus saw it. Adding to the problem, many important historic sites are in dispute, such as where Jesus was entombed. Roman Catholics and some other Christian persuasions believe he was entombed inside Jerusalem's walls and have built a large shrine over the site to commemorate the spot. Protestants contend that he was entombed outside Jerusalem's walls near the spot he was crucified, and have converted the site into a garden.

Still, much remains as it was when Jesus lived. In Old City Jerusalem, it is possible to walk some of the same narrow, cavernous stone streets that he walked. Outside the city, the hills and caves, both those near the roads and in the distance, provide much the same view that Jesus saw. Shepherds still tend their flocks exactly as they did two millennia ago, on the same hillsides Jesus visited. The Dead Sea and its surroundings appear as desolate today as they did then. In Galilee, one can sit quietly on the hillside near the Sea of Galilee where Jesus is thought to have taught his disciples and see an expanse of water, fertile hills, and bare cliff sides very much as he saw them. While I was in the Holy Land, politics prevented visitors

Herod's Temple

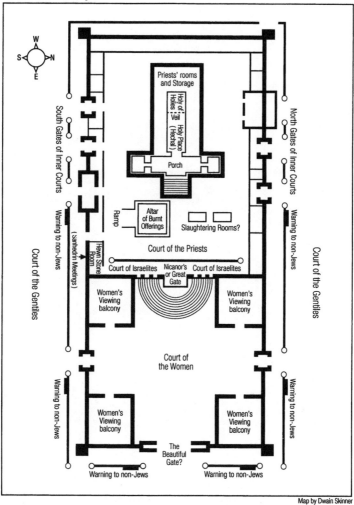

Map by Dwain Skinner

from getting near the River Jordan site where Jesus was baptized, but the ancient river was accessible farther to the north. Also, throughout the Holy Land, archeologists have excavated numerous ancient cities and other structures, providing ample settings to help me put Jesus' life into perspective for this book.

However, the point of this book is not how closely it adheres to literal fact. Neither is the point of this book whether Jesus was the Messiah, or the Son of God, or God himself as many believe he was. The point of this book is *The Gospel of Yeshua.*

Introduction

More than two thousand years before Jesus was born, people worshiped a plethora of gods. The problem was that none of the gods seemed any more powerful than any of the others. None stood out. All of them promised, but none delivered.

Then, according to the book of Genesis, a nomad named Abram, who lived in the city of Ur, in what became the present-day state of Iraq, discovered that by looking deeply within himself he could detect a profound voice speaking to him. Abram listened to that voice, communed with it, learned he could trust it implicitly, and affirmed it as the one true God.

The story is told that when Abram was seventy-five, he heard God tell him to leave his home and go to a land that God would show him. God promised Abram he would bless him personally by making his name great, bless him on a broader scale by making of him a great nation, and bless him indirectly by blessing all the people of the world through him. Abram obeyed the call and, taking his wife, nephew, servants, and personal possessions, followed a meandering path that eventually led them into the land of Canaan, in what is now the Holy Land.

Years later, when Abraham (God's new name for Abram) was alleged to be ninety-nine, God told him that he and his wife, Sarah, who was elderly and barren, would have a son, and her son's children would become a great nation. When Abraham told Sarah, she laughed. She thought it was ludicrous. But several years later, Sarah gave birth to Isaac.

For 500 years, the descendants of Abraham and Sarah prospered throughout Canaan as they began building the nation God had promised. Mostly they lived in the south country of Judea, in the pasture lands between Hebron and Be'ersheva, but then a famine swept through the land and forced them to move to Egypt.

At first the Egyptians welcomed them, but in 1500 B.C.E. a new king arose in Egypt, canceled their welcome and enslaved them. The king and his successors kept the people enslaved for 250 years until, in 1250 B.C.E., Moses, trusting God just as Abraham had, led them out of slavery, across the Red Sea, and to freedom in the Sinai Desert.

For many years, the people wandered in the desert region, with Moses ensconced as their undisputed leader. Moses taught them of a single God who wanted to give them a land of their own, the same land he had given Abraham, a land beautiful beyond their imaginations — he called it "a land flowing with milk and honey" — if they would follow him and do his will.

Moses reminded the people how God had demonstrated his power throughout their history. God had promised the elderly nomad, Abram, that Abram would father a nation, and Abram did. God had promised to free the people from slavery in Egypt, and he did.

Now, Moses told them, God was making a new promise. He was promising them a land of their own if they would fulfill his requirements — which Moses said were to live harmoniously with God, treat one another justly, and live together in brotherly kindness.

The people elected to trust Moses' teaching and follow the

God he taught them about, and soon they began to feel they were being given unique insights into the nature of God. The feeling grew so strong that they began to believe that God had chosen them to be his special people. They even entered a binding covenant with God. The covenant was expressed as, "I will be your God and you will be my people."

Moses went up onto Mount Sinai and brought down what he said were commandments God had written in stone to outline the life he wanted his people to live.

God also commanded the people to build a tabernacle for him to live in, giving them detailed instructions on how it should be built. The people built the tabernacle and they moved it with them wherever they went. Any time they set up a new camp in the wilderness, they made the tabernacle the camp's central focus.

During those years of wandering, the people developed into a nation of twelve tribes. Then, about 1,200 years before Jesus was born, Moses' successor, Joshua, led them across the Jordan River near Jericho and returned them to Canaan, the same land that God had given Abram to start a nation. The Canaanites, Philistines, and others who occupied the land tried to keep them out, but the Jews defeated them and gained a foothold in the area.

When Joshua died, much land remained unconquered, so the various tribes sent out expeditions on their own. Some succeeded, some did not, and as a result the tribes sometimes became separated from one another. This weakened them militarily and enabled the strong, pirate-like Philistines to extend their rule over the whole center and south of Palestine.

The people began demanding a king be named to weld the disorganized tribes into a whole. Samuel, the last of the judges and first of the prophets, vigorously opposed the idea, but when the people insisted, Samuel acquiesced. The other prophets consented and Saul was chosen as Israel's first king.

Saul's armies gradually regained the highlands of Judea and

Jerusalem

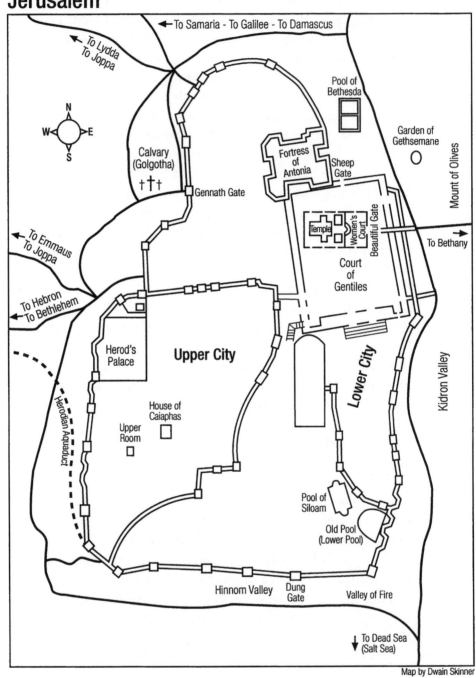

To Samaria - To Galilee - To Damascus

To Lydda
To Joppa

Pool of
Bethesda

Garden of
Gethsemane

N
W — E
S

Calvary
(Golgotha)

Fortress
of
Antonia

Sheep
Gate

Mount of Olives

† † †

Gennath Gate

Temple

Women's
Court

Beautiful Gate

To Emmaus
To Joppa

To Bethany

Court
of
Gentiles

To Hebron
To Bethlehem

Herod's
Palace

Upper City

Lower City

Kidron Valley

Herodian Aquaduct

House of
Caiaphas

Upper
Room

Pool of
Siloam

Old Pool
(Lower Pool)

Hinnom Valley

Dung
Gate

Valley of Fire

To Dead Sea
(Salt Sea)

Map by Dwain Skinner

the center of Palestine from the Philistines. However, in about 1017 B.C.E., Saul was killed during a battle in the Jezreel Valley. David succeeded him as king, and around 1000 B.C.E. David defeated the Philistines and surrounding peoples, then made victory complete by conquering the city of Jerusalem and making the area around Mount Zion his capital.

Forty years later, David's son Solomon inherited the throne and built a magnificent temple in Jerusalem as a permanent home for the God who had led them there. The permanent temple, which replaced the portable tabernacle, is believed to have stood on a platform ten feet tall, and ten steps led to an entrance that was flanked by two large stone pillars. Thousands of laborers were needed to erect it, but once finished it stood as the home of God, an eternal reminder of what he had done for his chosen people, and the central place of worship for Jews everywhere.

During the reigns of David and Solomon, the soon-to-be kingdom of Israel prospered and extended its control over a wide swath of land that was bordered on the west by the Mediterranean Sea, on the east by the desert beyond the Jordan Valley, on the north by the Land of the Phoenicians (roughly the present-day Lebanon and Syria), and on the south by the Sinai Desert.

Great spiritual growth accompanied both David's and Solomon's reigns. Oral traditions concerning the patriarchs, the sojourn in Egypt, the Exodus from Egypt, and the giving of the Law were brought together in written form that would shape the religion of Judaism for centuries to come.

After Solomon died, in 922 B.C.E., ten of the twelve tribes revolted against King Rehoboam and formed the northern kingdom of Israel. Judah became the southern kingdom. The split weakened them both and made them easier prey for their common enemies, of which there were many because Palestine was too important geographically to be left alone. Palestine was at the crossroads of the known world, so virtually all international commerce, both civilian and military, had to pass through it. The Jordan Valley and the Mediterranean coastline formed wide, flat, natural highways for north-south traffic, and the Jezreel and Turan valleys in Galilee provided the easiest east-west crossover routes anywhere in the world. The two valleys' junction in Galilee formed one of the world's busiest crossroads. Many countries and kingdoms wanted to control it for their own purposes.

In 722 B.C.E., the Assyrians destroyed the northern kingdom and, in 587 B.C.E., the Babylonians destroyed the southern kingdom, including Jerusalem and Solomon's temple, and took the people into captivity. These crises gave rise to some of Judaism's greatest prophets, among them Isaiah, Ezekiel, and Jeremiah, who constantly pleaded with the people to stop straying and fulfill their covenant with God.

The Jews returned from Babylonian captivity in 537 B.C.E., but the nation was not to reach its earlier grandeur. At times it had autonomy, and the people built a smaller version of the temple on the temple mount. Nevertheless, the inescapable fact of daily life continued to be foreign domination or outright rule by other nations.

By 400 B.C.E., the Torah (the Jewish bible's first five books, generally accepted as having been written by Moses) was completed, solidifying in writing what, until then, had been mostly oral tradition. By then the Jewish religion had ten basic pillars:

Monotheism: The keystone of the Jewish faith, and one of Judaism's greatest contributions to humanity, was the idea that God is one. The heart and soul of Judaism was expressed in the words of the *Shema:* "Hear, O Israel, the Lord is our God, the Lord is one."

Chosen People: Jews believed God had chosen them to be his special people. At first they accepted this as a great honor, but in time they came to see it as a grave responsibility.

Covenant: The covenant—"I will be your God and you will be my people"—was a binding agreement between God and the Jews. The exodus from slavery in Egypt, during which the people came to believe God had chosen them, and the covenant, which followed, formed and defined Israel's history.

The Law: The Law stated the conditions for the covenant and described the life of a person in covenant with God. In its earliest stages, the entire Law was contained in the first five books of the Bible, but later it came to include much tradition as well.

Sacrifice: The people discovered early that keeping the covenant with God was impossible because regardless of how hard they tried they constantly broke it and, therefore, their relationship with God. A means was needed to restore the relationship, and sacrifice became that means. But since human sacrifice obviously would be self-destroying, animal sacrifice was substituted. (Some form of sacrifice is an important part of most religions.)

The Temple: The temple, in Jerusalem, was Judaism's primary religious shrine. It was built to be the home of God, and therefore it was the only building in the world in which animal sacrifices to God could be carried out. It was also the central place of worship, prayer, and study for Jews worldwide.

Synagogues: When the people were away from the temple they gathered in local synagogues ("congregations") to worship, pray, and study together.

Prophets: The main function of the prophets ("those inspired by God") was to speak for God. They warned against disobedience and unfaithfulness, called the people back into their covenant relationship with God, and declared the will of God in specific situations. Historians believe the time of the prophets ended by 400 B.C.E.

Reign of God: Jews believed that God would intervene to end the intolerable misery of their earthly existence and establish his reign on earth. They expected a period of woe would be followed by a great judgment, after which Israel, with its religious and political capital in Jerusalem, would become the center of the world.

Messiah: Some believed God would intervene directly, but most thought he would first send an agent, a Messiah ("anointed one"), to inaugurate his reign. How the Messiah would manifest was open to wide variations of opinion.

Persia ruled Israel from 450 B.C.E. to 330 B.C.E. Then, Alexander the Great, as part of his effort to spread Hellenistic culture throughout the world, forced the Persians out of Palestine and made the Jews subjects of Greece. That lasted for about 150 years, during which time a number of Jews began adopting Greek customs and falling away from their own religious practices. Most orthodox Jews thought that trend was abhorrent because they believed the Law was perfect and everlasting, and the purpose of life was to obey the Law absolutely. They were so certain of the utter rightness of their cause that a number of them publicly separated themselves from everyone else so they could devote all their waking hours to demonstrating their religion. Their main purpose in life became obeying the Law publicly, and in meticulous detail, for all to see. They became known as the Pharisees, which means "separated ones."

Early in their development, however, the Pharisees realized it was impossible to obey the Law because it was often vague and open to interpretation. For instance, the Law forbade work on the Sabbath but it did not define work. How could a Pharisee know if he was working on the Sabbath if he did not know what work was?

To solve the dilemma, a group known as the scribes developed. It became the scribes' duty to study and interpret the Law so that all Pharisees could know exactly what they had to do, and avoid doing, to please God.

The scribes accomplished their task in astounding detail. They classified all work into thirty-nine categories, then established countless rules to cover every situation that could conceivably exist within each category. They declared that walking more than 200 cubits (about 300 feet) constituted traveling, and traveling constituted work. Therefore, it was all right for a

Pharisee to walk 200 cubits on a Sabbath, but walking any farther than 200 cubits was to disobey God. Similarly, the scribes declared that wearing ribbons in one's hair constituted carrying a burden, and carrying a burden constituted work. Therefore, women could wear ribbons in their hair six days a week, but on a Sabbath it was a sin. The scribes established literally thousands of such rules. The Pharisees—normally intelligent, substantial, well-meaning, middle-class and, by their lights, devoutly religious people — devoted themselves to memorizing those rules and living their days in strict obedience to them.

But it didn't end there. In time, most Pharisees began treating the scribes' interpretation of the Law as if the interpretation were more authoritative, more binding and more important than the Law itself. The interpretation became more important even than God. The result was that in the process of praising God, many Pharisees lost God. Without intending to, they came to mock the very God they so loudly professed to serve.

Because they were so fervent in demonstrating how religious they were, they gained great power within the temple's hierarchy. Eventually their strength inside the temple became second only to that of the Sadducees, who represented the elite of Jewish society.

The Sadducees came from the aristocratic, landowning, priestly families, and their lives centered around the temple. They also largely controlled the conduct of political affairs in Palestine by controlling the Sanhedrin, which was the supreme court of Judaism. The Sadducees made up a solid majority of the Sanhedrin (the Pharisees were second), so they usually got whatever they wanted. Normally, that suited the Pharisees well, for though the Pharisees and Sadducees had some theological differences, they both profited handsomely from the temple system, and so both adamantly opposed any change in the status quo.

About 150 years before Jesus was born, Alexander's successors tried to stamp out the Jewish religion entirely, but the Jews

Israel

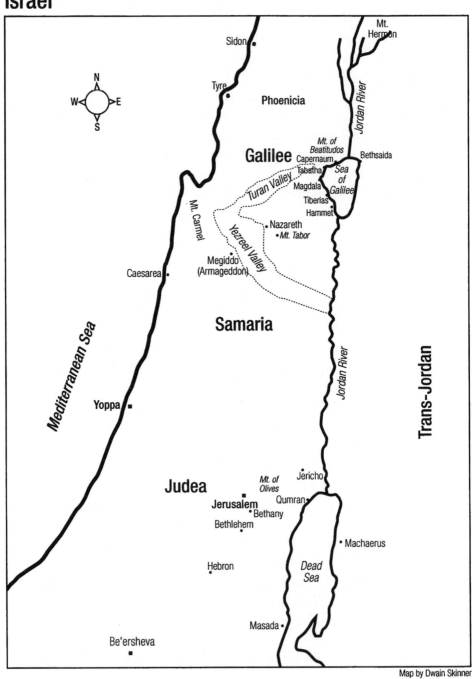

Map by Dwain Skinner

rebelled with such fury that they earned for themselves a century of precarious freedom. At the end of that century, about sixty years before Jesus was born, Pompey marched into Jerusalem at the head of a Roman column and conquered Palestine for the Roman Empire.

In many ways, the Roman Empire, which was just coming into its fullest power, was good for Palestine, as it was for the rest of the world it controlled. Rome kept the land routes and sea lanes open and safe, established an equitable system of justice, and provided services for the people. And, so long as the people paid their taxes and caused no trouble, Rome allowed them a great deal of freedom, including religious freedom.

However, the taxes were cripplingly steep and the freedom was illusory. The taxes, added to the temple's endless ecclesiastical collections, constituted a huge burden on the people, especially the "people of the land," or the common people. The temple demanded ten percent of all a person had, then added mandatory offerings for such things as widows, children, animals, and the poor. Rome had a long list of its own taxes, including poll taxes, salt taxes, crown taxes (on the heads of brides and bridegrooms), land taxes, cattle taxes, city taxes, road taxes, frontier taxes. Widespread corruption among tax collectors, many of them Jews who often pocketed part of their collections, made matters even worse. The massive offerings, taxes, and corruption took their toll and contributed to a widespread, grinding poverty that permeated the land.

Worse than the poverty was the lack of freedom. Ever since its beginning, there had always been another kingdom or nation wanting to conquer and control Palestine. The Roman Empire was merely the latest and the most powerful. Regardless of the privileges granted them, the people were not free.

Nevertheless, the Sadducees supported Rome. Because the Sadducees were mostly interested in maintaining their privileged lifestyles, and Rome was mostly interested in maintaining peace, the two sides arrived at a compromise. Rome allowed the Sadducees to keep their precious status quo in return for causing Rome no problems. The Sadducees thus became cozy with their Roman conquerors and grew wealthy while the "people of the land" lived in poverty.

Most of the people of the land hated living under a foreign power, but there was nothing they could do about it. They were as powerless as they were poor. The Sadducees and Pharisees looked down on them with contempt, and they had no political voice, no economic power, and no outside support — except from their God, to whom, more and more, they looked for help.

Specifically, they began looking for a Messiah. God had promised them a Messiah. Their prophets had predicted a Messiah. Now the people began expecting one. They disagreed over exactly what they thought the Messiah would be or do, but most expected him to be a warrior-king who would destroy Israel's enemies, judge the world, and establish God's earthly reign with its capital in Jerusalem.

About forty years before Jesus was born, Caesar Augustus appointed Herod, a half-Jewish friend of Rome, as a puppet king of Judea. Herod, who became known as Herod the Great, ruled with a cruel and merciless hand. As the years passed, he became increasingly suspicious and violent until it reached the point of madness. He murdered many of his political rivals, real or imagined. He even murdered three of his own sons because he thought, with no proof, they had turned against him.

His madness reached its depth soon after Jesus was born. Some astrologers told him a child born in Bethlehem would grow up to become a king, so Herod, wanting to protect his throne, responded by ordering his troops to kill all male children in Bethlehem who were less than two years old.

Not long after that, Herod died and Palestine was split into three sections, which were divided among Herod's three living sons. Archelaeus was given power over Judea, including Jerusalem, but he was so brutal and so incompetent that the people in

Jerusalem revolted. To get better control over the territory, Caesar put it under Roman governors (procurators), who were directly answerable to Rome. That, however, only made the Jews' hatred of Rome burn with an even hotter flame, especially in Galilee where the people were known for their spirit of independence.

But the people had no power. Rome had it all — political, economic, and military — and it used its power without mercy against any enemy, real or perceived. Public executions of those who would overthrow Rome became common street scenes, causing the people to pray even more fervently that God would soon send them the long-promised and long-sought Messiah. By the time Jesus turned thirty, the air was alive with expectation that the Messiah would arrive at any moment.

1

Snow, rain, and dew fall gently onto Mt. Herman and seep deeply into the ground. Near the foot of the mountain, the water emerges as springs. The springs quickly join together to form the narrow, shallow, meandering River Jordan.

The River Jordan flows southward for twenty-eight miles, through one lake, until, at nearly seven hundred feet below sea level, it pools as the Sea of Galilee, a nearly pear-shaped lake that measures thirteen miles long by eight miles wide and reaches depths of one hundred fifty feet. The lake teems with bass, trout, catfish, talapia, sardines, and some twenty other varieties of fish.

On most days, the lake rests serenely on the valley floor between the steep, mostly bare, yellow-brown valley walls that rise sharply from both sides. On other days, cool dry winds sweep down from the mountains and clash with the warm moist air over the water, producing violent storms that erupt suddenly and thrash the calm waters into angry, dangerous waves.

At the southern tip of the lake, the River Jordan spills over the lake's banks and resumes its flow southward through the valley toward the Dead Sea. Averaging about five feet deep and thirty feet wide, the muddy little river ambles along a tightly winding path that leads it through citrus groves and other semi-tropical landscapes while billowing willow trees drape their limbs over the water in great profusion. The river meanders two hundred miles between the Sea of Galilee and the Dead Sea, although the direct distance is only sixty-five miles.

At approximately 1,300 feet below sea level, the Jordan empties into the Dead Sea, from which there is no outlet. Water escapes from it only by evaporation. The sea covers 390 square miles, is 1,200 feet deep, and is the lowest spot on earth. It contains many times the salt of any other sea or ocean in the world, but no life. Its salts permeate the surrounding earth so thoroughly that a lifeless, dusty, rock-strewn, cave-pocked wilderness stretches miles from it in all directions.

A few miles upstream from the Dead Sea, where willow branches still bow over the Jordan River, a man stands waist deep in the muddy water. His name is John. Temple rulers in Jerusalem recognize John as a priest due to his birth line, which automatically makes him one. He is a descendant of Jacob, father of the nation Israel, and a son of Zacharias, a priest in good standing in the temple.

But John does not act like a temple priest. He lives like a wild man in the desert. He is about thirty, lean, taut, hard, austere, stern. He exists by eating wild honey he finds in the wilderness and the bitter, purple-black locusts that hang in thick pods from trees. He wears a garment made from camel hair, clenching it around his waist with a leather belt. There is wildness in his eyes, urgency in his manner.

John spends his nights praying and meditating, and his days preaching and baptizing. He preaches boldly and loudly against evil wherever he finds it, whether it be among ordinary Jews, the temple rulers, or King Herod Antipas. He censures ordinary Jews for living as if God does not matter, or for assuming they are safe from God's judgment just because they are God's chosen people. He berates the temple rulers for putting their own comforts ahead of their covenant with God. He savages King Herod for divorcing his wife to marry his brother's wife, and then living with her in open adultery. Herod's spokesmen have warned John many times to cease his attacks on the king, but their warnings only spur John to savage the king's immorality even more fiercely.

Just as fiercely as he reviles his listeners, though, he fervently calls them to remember they are children of God.

"Stop neglecting God," he cries out to them. "Turn away from the false gods you're worshiping — money, power, lust, whatever it is you put first in your life. Return to your covenant with God so that he can forgive you and you can live joyously.

"Repent!" he shouts to them, angrily and pleadingly, desperately, over and over. "The reign of God is near!"

John also offers to baptize his listeners in the river as a sign that God of their fathers forgives them for failing or refusing to honor their promise to be his people, and also as a sign that they will put God first in their lives.

The baptizing has grown to be so popular that John has

become known throughout Judea as John the Baptist. The crowds flock to him. His baptisms and his preaching fuel their deepest hopes that the long-awaited Messiah will arrive soon. Some of John's admirers, a growing number, even whisper that John may be the Messiah.

None of this is lost on the temple rulers in Jerusalem, who increasingly look upon John with deep suspicion. For one thing, John baptizes Jews with water, and Jews don't need to be baptized with water. Gentiles converting to Judaism need to be baptized with water because they are considered unclean and must have their sins washed away before they can be accepted, but Jews are God's chosen people. As such they are born clean and do not need baptizing beyond infant circumcision.

Of much more concern to the temple rulers is the rising perception among the rabble that John might be the Messiah. One of the most important duties of the Jews' supreme court, the Sanhedrin, is to deal with anyone suspected of being a false prophet — and John's actions have definitely raised that suspicion.

To learn for certain what they're dealing with, the Sanhedrin sends a delegation of Sadducees and Pharisees to the river's edge this day to question John. John recognizes the delegation members as soon as he sees them, and immediately perceives why they are here.

"You brood of vipers!" he bellows at them. He hurls more invectives at them as they approach, but the delegation blandly ignores his words and begins questioning.

"Are you the Messiah?" one asks.

"No," John replies. "I am not the Messiah, but, if you only knew, the Messiah is here."

The delegation member persists: "Many Jews believe the prophet Elijah will return shortly before the Messiah appears and will prepare the world to receive him. Are you Elijah?"

"I am not."

"Moses said that before the Messiah arrives, God will raise up the greatest prophet ever, but there hasn't been a prophet for 400 years. Are you the expected new prophet?"

"I am not."

"Then who are you?"

John takes a deep breath, then shouts so all will hear: "I am only the voice of one crying out in the wilderness, 'Make straight the way of the Lord!'"

"But if you are not the Messiah, Elijah or the prophet," comes the calm reply, "then why do you baptize as you do?"

"I baptize with water," John roars back, "but one who is more powerful than I is coming after me. I am not worthy to carry his sandals. He will baptize you with the Holy Spirit and fire!"

The Sadducees and Pharisees are not satisfied, but they ignore his insults and accept his answers for the moment. They will discuss them with their superiors in Jerusalem later, then decide what, if anything, to do. For now, they turn and leave as abruptly as they arrived.

The next day, as John is preaching and baptizing large crowds of people, he looks up and sees a tall, powerful-looking man about his own age standing on the river's bank. The man's dark hair and thick beard frame intensely warm, bright eyes that at this moment are laughing.

"Yeshua," John whispers. Then, with a sudden burst of glad enthusiasm, he thunders: "Yeshua!"

Yeshua laughs aloud and starts down the hillside as John eagerly splashes out of the water and runs to greet his first cousin, closest friend, and, though six months younger than John, his spiritual mentor. The two embrace in a great bear-hug. Then John steps back and looks at Yeshua.

"Welcome! But what brings you here from Nazareth?"

"I come so that you can baptize me."

"No!" John's retort is immediate, unsmiling and adamant.

"Why not?"

"Because you're the teacher. I'm only the pupil! It is you who should baptize me."

But Yeshua is just as adamant. "You must baptize me, John," he says patiently.

John hesitates, confused. "I don't understand," he says. "Ever since we were children you've been the leader. You're the smart one. You always shared your knowledge and wisdom with me, but you're the teacher. I can't baptize my teacher."

"Yes, you can. And you must. John, you know as well as anyone that I've spent my life studying God's word, and if I've learned anything it is that God does what God says God will do. He never fails."

"I know that. It was your teaching of that that started me on this ministry."

Yeshua nods. "Yes, and soon I'll be starting my own ministry. I've offered God everything I have or am — physical, mental, or spiritual. I'll do whatever God wants, regardless of what

I think of it and regardless of the consequences. I'm ready to begin now, but first I need to feel cleansed of all that is past. I need a fresh beginning. I need you to baptize me."

"But. . . ."

"Let it be so now," Yeshua says reassuringly as he reaches out and lays his hand on John's shoulder. "It is right."

John looks at his cousin a long moment, then slowly shakes his head in surrender.

"I do not understand you, but if you insist. . . ."

"I insist."

John takes Yeshua by the arm and leads him into the water until they are nearly chest deep, then leans him backward until Yeshua is totally immersed in the river. As Yeshua goes under, he prays for forgiveness of his shortcomings, and pledges afresh to fully use whatever talents he has to serve God in whatever way God wants.

Then, as John lifts him from the water, the sky suddenly seems to split apart, and a wave of love more powerful than anything Yeshua has ever imagined descends on him with the gentleness of a dove. Yeshua feels as though the spirit of God himself is descending on him. As the wave passes through him, a loud, clear voice rings out in his head:

"You are my beloved son, and with you I am well pleased."

And then, as suddenly as the experience began, it ends. The sky is whole again, the wave of love is gone, and the voice is silent. The whole episode lasted only a few seconds.

Yeshua is stunned. In the past, he has experienced God's closeness many times and in many ways, but never like this. He has never even imagined anything like this. He doesn't know what has happened; he only knows that whatever happened was real, powerful, and, somehow, it has changed his life permanently and profoundly.

Yeshua tries to focus his eyes on John, who is staring back at him with astonishment. John felt Yeshua's shock as he rose from the water, and he sees the dazed look in Yeshua's eyes now.

John has baptized countless people and many of them have reacted strongly, but he has never witnessed anything like this.

"What happened?" John blurts.

But Yeshua can only shake his head. He cannot answer. He is too overwhelmed to speak. Instead, he waves John off and makes his way to the river's bank. As John returns his attention to the crowds, Yeshua finds a solitary spot among the willow trees where he collapses to the ground and sits in silence, hands clasped, head bowed. He tries to pray, but is too overwhelmed to pray. He can't pray, can't think, can't do anything. He needs time to be alone and clear his head so he can think. He needs time *now!*

2

Yeshua stands up and looks to the river where John has resumed baptizing others. He signals to John that he is leaving, and, before John can attempt to talk with him, he half walks, half stumbles into a wilderness that seems to stretch into forever.

He wanders aimlessly for hours — he doesn't know how many — until he drops from exhaustion and falls into a fitful, dreamless sleep. When he awakes, the baptism experience still burns within him with a ferocity that will not fade. He cannot force it away. Cannot rest. The memory is too strong, too recent — too real.

He wants to be quiet and contemplate what has happened, meditate on it, but he cannot still his mind.

He wanders again, stumbles again, collapses again. He covers himself in the shade of a rock and tries to sleep.

Sometimes he slips into an uneasy unconsciousness, but whenever he awakens the memory is still there, as powerful as ever.

He wanders farther. He does not eat, and his sleep is not

peaceful, but as time passes, his mind begins to calm. As it does, he fights asking the question that must be answered——a question too ludicrous to consider, too blasphemous to speak, but too important to ignore. He is surprised, therefore, when, while he sits and stares into the sky, he hears his mouth almost whisper the words slowly and quietly:

"Am . . . I . . . the . . . Messiah?"

He tells himself he cannot be. But when he removes his pride and considers the question objectively, he knows it is possible that he is. The baptismal experience may be the crowning event and the most powerful evidence, but long before that there were other indications.

He fits the criteria, meager as they are. According to Scripture, the Messiah will be a descendant of King David, and Yeshua is a descendant of David through his father's bloodline. But more than that, Yeshua has always known he is special in other ways. Beginning as far back as he can remember, and lasting all his life, compared with his peers he has always been the strongest, the fastest, the smartest, the quickest, the cleverest, the most knowledgeable, the wisest. He has never known an equal by any criterion. No one has ever been as good as he at anything. And spiritual matters have been foremost in his mind since he was a child.

So now, if he looks objectively at himself, he has to ask: *If there is to be a Messiah, why not me? And if not me, who?*

Yeshua sighs heavily, then laughs aloud as he considers the absurdity of it all: He, an undistinguished carpenter from an undistinguished family from an undistinguished village, is actually wandering the wilderness wondering if he is the Messiah.

He can't tell whether he is being unthinkably arrogant or

blatantly honest, but nevertheless here he sits, seriously considering the possibility.

For days the question burns unanswered. Yeshua keeps wandering and wondering, but there are no more religious experiences to inspire him, no more voices from heaven to guide him, and nothing but the desert to accompany him. He is alone with his memories and his thoughts.

There is no respite for him. No guidance. No answers. But this cannot go on forever. He knows he must find an answer soon and move on.

He leans back against a rock, rubs his temples, closes his eyes, and lets his mind wander over his life. What led him to this astonishing place? And what should he do about it?

He had been born thirty years earlier in Bethlehem, a tiny Palestinian village just south of Jerusalem, the first son of Mary and Joseph, a carpenter. Soon after he was born, some astrologers told King Herod that a male child born recently in Bethlehem would grow up to be king. To protect his throne, Herod ordered his guards to kill all males in Bethlehem who were less than two years old. Yeshua's parents rushed him out safely ahead of Herod's wrath and took him to Egypt, where they remained until Herod died and Joseph felt it was safe to return to Palestine. Then he led his family to Nazareth, a mountaintop town in Galilee, about seventy-five miles north of Jerusalem.

Nazareth was an undistinguished little town that sat in a shallow bowl atop the 2,000-foot-tall Nazareth Mountain, so when Yeshua looked out over his neighbor's roofs he could see only the ridges of nearby hills against the sky.

His house in Nazareth was like all other houses in the village. Its walls were made of rocks sealed with mud, its roof was made of tree limbs daubed with mud, and it was built in the form of an upside-down and backward L with its two inner sides cupping a rock patio.

The natural beauty of the land around him — the vineyards, the citrus groves, the olive gardens — masked the brutal reality of daily life among the people of the land in Galilee: relentless poverty. Many of the people Yeshua grew up with lived daily on the edge of economic disaster. Many went to bed at night not knowing where their next morning's breakfast would come from.

Some lived so precariously that a single drought, a single illness, could ruin them forever. Poverty persisted even though employment was plentiful. There were tradesmen, fishermen, government officials, merchants, and a few people of wealth. Nevertheless, Palestine was mostly an agricultural nation where most people eked out meager livings by working on the small farms. What little they did earn was largely claimed by either Rome or the temple.

Soon after Yeshua was born, Herod died, and Palestine was divided among his three sons. The Jews revolted, so Caesar put the territory under Roman procurators (governors) who were directly answerable to Rome.

That only made the Jews hate Roman rule even more, especially in the Galilee region where Yeshua lived. The Galileans were known for their spirit of independence as well as their unmistakable brogue. Malcontents and spies filled Galilee's streets. Especially powerful were the Zealots, radicals who would follow anyone they thought might lead in overthrowing Rome. Public executions became common scenes throughout the region where Yeshua lived.

Through all the turmoil, Joseph and Mary made certain all their children received the best education life in Nazareth would allow. The most important building in Nazareth was its synagogue, which doubled as the central place of worship and learning. Yeshua attended the school there, where he and his classmates learned by memorizing Scriptures a rabbi read them, then listening while the rabbi explained the meaning.

Yeshua did well in school. He had a natural, unquenchable thirst for knowledge and understanding, and he endlessly barraged his teachers with questions about the Scriptures and the issues they raised. He learned quickly and thoroughly, and he remembered what he learned. By the time he was thirteen, he had exceeded his rabbis' ability to teach him. Once, when his parents took him to Jerusalem for a religious festival, he engaged the temple's wisest rabbis in conversation and astounded them with his knowledge and understanding of spiritual matters.

After Yeshua returned to Nazareth from the festival, he began teaching adults in the synagogue, and, despite his age, quickly became one of the synagogue's most popular teachers. He learned carpentry and masonry by working in his father's shop, and often accompanied his father or other townsmen on trips to Capernaum on the Sea of Galilee's northern shore.

Yeshua especially liked Capernaum. He grew up fishing the lake with others who lived near there, particularly two sets of brothers who were to become professional fishermen on the lake: his cousins John and James, and their friends Peter and Andrew.

Mostly, Yeshua liked the atmosphere of Capernaum. In stark

contrast to Nazareth, which was composed entirely of orthodox Jews, Capernaum was populated with both Jews and gentiles.

During one of their trips to Capernaum, Joseph explained
to Yeshua the reason for the unusual setting:

"Seven springs near Capernaum feed warm water into the
Sea of Galilee. In winter months, the warm water attracts an
abundance of fish — especially talapia, which love warm water
— and the fish attract fishermen from throughout the area.
Jews mostly live to the west of Capernaum and gentiles live
mostly to the east, but the fish draw them all here regardless of
their backgrounds or cultures, and they live and work peacefully together."

The presence of Jews and gentiles living and working together peacefully added a dimension that Yeshua liked. Life there
seemed to be for everyone, not just the Jews.

As Yeshua grew toward adulthood, it became apparent that
the Nazarene rabbis could no longer provide the depth and
breadth of knowledge his limitless curiosity demanded. He developed an increasing need for new teachers, new ideas, fresh
approaches.

And he found them all, almost literally, at his doorstep.

If he were to walk south from his house and climb up to the
lip of the bowl in which Nazareth sat, he could peer over the
ridge's crest and look down upon one of the busiest, most important international highways in the world: the Jezreel Valley.
Furthermore, fewer than five miles to his west was the Jezreel's
hugely important junction with the just-as-busy Turan Valley.

Yeshua had always loved the beauty of the view. He could
look directly across the valley's twenty-mile-wide expanse and

see the ancient fortress city of Megiddo (which the Jews called Armageddon) gleaming atop the southern mountain range. Or he could look down to the valley's flat floor, which lay at sea level 2,000 feet below him, and see the quiet, slow-moving little Kishon River. Square green patches of cultivated fields jutted raggedly out from the Kishon and framed its route eastward toward its eventual junction with the Jordan River.

The panorama also provided a rich view of Israel's history. There was the plain of Esdraelon, where Deborah and Barak fought, where Gideon won his victories, where Saul crashed to disaster and Josiah died in battle. There was Naboth's vineyard and the place where Jehu slaughtered Jezebel. There was Shunem, where Elisha had lived, and Carmel, where Elijah had fought an epic battle with the prophets of Baal.

What mattered most to Yeshua as he matured was the enormous variety of merchants, royalty, military men, religious leaders, and other international travelers who moved through the valleys in an endless stream. It was a simple matter for Yeshua to slip down the mountainside, walk into the valley and converse with people of all colors, nationalities and religious beliefs. He had learned how to communicate with foreign travelers during a lifetime of accompanying his father and other Nazarenes on their trips to Capernaum, for the shortest and easiest route between Nazareth and Capernaum was the Turan Valley, where he could walk and talk with an endless mélange of foreigners.

As Yeshua grew older, he would descend the mountainside by day and search out the wisest religious and philosophical travelers he could find; then he would sit with them by their campfires and talk late into the night about spiritual matters.

He wanted to compare their religious ideas with his own so he could understand clearly how they differed and how they agreed. He wanted to test his ideas against others.

Sometimes his bottomless curiosity drove him to foreign lands, where he sought out wise spiritual leaders to teach him their ways. He explored the world's great religions, but also many other lesser-known systems of faith from far-flung lands.

And the more he studied, the more he marveled at how similar all developed religions were at their core. They differed in their rituals, customs, and other expressions, but at their core they shared one crucial trait: the necessity of love. Almost all the philosophies that Yeshua studied, even the secular systems of thought, were grounded to some degree in love, regardless of what the religion or its gods were called, or what its rituals were.

That realization slowly planted a thought in Yeshua's heart and mind that was utterly new to humanity: If the God of his fathers was the God of love, and the God of love was the creator and sustainer of all people everywhere, then all persons on earth were truly brothers and sisters. They were members of a single family, all children of one loving God — regardless of any differences in their locales, languages, color, sex, beliefs, rituals, creeds, or anything else. Geography, weather, economics, and many other factors over several millennia had produced many approaches to an unseen god or gods, but love had remained the one constant. Yeshua's understanding of the deity did not contradict the God of his fathers, but neither was his fathers' religion big enough to hold his growing understanding.

By the time Yeshua turned thirty he had decided that he wanted to dedicate the remainder of his life to serving the God he had come to know so intimately. That decision had led him to John, the Jordan River, and his stunning baptism.

And now he wanders the wilderness, wondering if he is the Messiah.

Time eventually begins to wear away the impact of his baptism and, despite the dizzying awe he still feels, he begins to relax and think. He realizes he cannot stay in the wilderness forever; he must come to terms with his experience and plan what to do.

But first he must know if he is the Messiah. If so, what does it mean, and what is he to do about it?

He cannot decide. The questions are too important and the information is too scant. Yet decisions must be made. Now that his mind is calming, Yeshua employs a method for meditating that he learned from holy men in the Yezreel Valley and during his travels. He learned many methods designed to relax a person so deeply he can cease even to think, yet keep his mind so alert he can absorb whatever wisdom the universe has to offer — a wisdom he has come to trust, as Abraham did, as the voice of God.

Yeshua has used the method many times while sitting alone on the Nazareth Mountain on which he lived, and on the neighboring and more sparsely populated Mount Tabor.

As evening nears, as the sun's silver begins to melt toward gold, he sits quietly in the desert. He puts the sun to his left, folds his legs in front of him and rests his hands by his side, palms facing up. He sits perfectly erect, the straightness of his spine perpendicular to gravity, as if he were dangling from a thread strung through his head and spine. He closes his eyes, sways slightly, then allows his weight to settle naturally, lightly, limply, upon his body's frame.

From the depth of his soul he prays that he may silence his

own desires, transcend the awareness of his body, cease even to think, so that his mind, heart, and soul can open to the universe.

He sits quietly and motionless for a few minutes, then breathes in deeply and slowly, holds his breath for a few seconds, and exhales slowly. He repeats this ritual several times, always breathing deeply and slowly. As he begins to slip into a deeper state of relaxation, still sitting erect and motionless, he begins to emit what at first sounds like a slow moan.

"*Ohhhhhhhhh. . .*" he begins, his voice resonating deep within his diaphragm. He holds the sound steady a few seconds while he feels the vibrations deep within him. Then, slowly, he seamlessly melts the sound into:

"*. . .Rheeeeeeeee . . .*" As the sound changes, the vibrations ascend from his diaphragm into his chest. Again he holds the sound steady for a few moments while he concentrates on the vibrations, then slowly blends it into:

"*. . .Ahhhhhhhhh . . .*" As he does, the vibrations rise higher, into his throat. A few moments there, and he simply closes his lips:

"*. . .mmmmmmmmm . . .*" The vibrations focus in his head now, and as he concentrates on them he slowly lifts his tongue to the roof of his mouth.

"*. . .nnnnnnnnn.*" The vibrations rise even higher and seem to exit through the top of his head.

As he finishes, he breathes in deeply again. Beginning with lungs full of fresh air, and again very slowly melting one syllable into the next, he repeats:

"*Ohhhhhhhhhrheeeeeeeeeeahhhhhhhhhmmmmmmmmmmnnnnnnnnn.*"

Again and again he emits the sounds, concentrating on the

vibrations as they begin deep within his diaphragm, rise through his chest and head, and seemingly exit through the top of his head, as if they were opening a channel through him to the universe beyond.

"Ohhhhhhhhhrrheeeeeeeeeahhhhhhhhhmmmmmmmmmmnnnnnnnnn."

As he repeats the sound, soon even thought itself begins to vanish from Yeshua's mind. When random thoughts pierce his awareness — thoughts of home, friends, his present situation — he notes them and lets them pass without judgment.

Now he sits quietly, motionless, listening intently and expectantly to the silence of the desert, a silence broken only by the sound of his own slow and rhythmic breathing. He feels his heart begin to beat more slowly.

He becomes less and less aware of his body, and soon he slips into a state of mind between wakefulness and sleep. His body sleeps, but his mind — unhinged from his physical body, unblocked by finite thinking, but still alert — roams the universe to receive whatever the universe offers. He will accept whatever comes without judging it, and evaluate it later.

Yeshua listens expectantly to the silence, and soon a soundless voice — the same voice Abraham heard? — wells up from deep within him. He listens intently to it, and very soon there is nothing in the universe except Yeshua and the voice within him.

Later, as the sun sets, Yeshua becomes aware that his mind is settling gently back into his body. He remains motionless for a long moment, eyes still closed, as he enjoys the easy sensation of a slow return.

A soft smile caresses his face. He does not know the answer to his burning question — "Am I the Messiah?" — but it no longer matters. The only thing that matters now, and it matters crucially, is that if there is any chance at all that he is the Messiah, then he owes it to God, the present and future world, and himself to trust the moment of his baptism and do the work of the Messiah — regardless of his own opinions, the costs, the consequences, or anything else.

Yeshua also realizes what that work is to be. He smiles at the realization, for in a sense he has known it since he was a child. He has heard it spelled out at least four times a day all his life. Rabbis lead congregational readings of the words twice daily, at morning and evening synagogue services; and his family also reads them together twice a day, every night just before sleep, and every morning just after waking.

The words are posted on the doorstep of his house, and on the doorstep of all Jews. They are among the most sacred words in all Judaism. They immediatly follow the *Shema*. And now, sitting in the desert as darkness gathers around him, Yeshua covers his eyes with his right hand, as his rabbis long ago taught him to do as an aide to concentration, and speaks words of the *V'Ahavta:*

"You shall love the Lord your God with all your heart, and with all your soul, and with all your might."

Such familiar words. Such ancient words. Words intended for all Jews — all people everywhere for that matter. But while Yeshua was listening to the voice deep within him he heard the words anew, and now he speaks them again. But this time he focuses on one of the words as he never had before:

" . . . *ALL!* your heart . . . *ALL!* your soul . . . *ALL!* Your strength."

The words flash like lightning and explode like thunder.

He feels his heart pound. The words are for everyone, but Yeshua sees in them now what God wants. God wants his Messiah to demonstrate the awesome power of absolute love by personifying that love *ABSOLUTELY!* God wants his Messiah to love so perfectly that everyone who looks at the Messiah will see a God who loves unconditionally, forgives readily, and is eager to commune with his children and give them whatever they need to make their lives joyous. God wants his Messiah to be as a crystal to focus that light. He wants him to be a catalyst for love.

Yeshua stares unseeing into the darkening sky. On its face, the thought of giving God *EVERYTHING!* seems absurd. How could any person possibly devote *ALL!* his talents and energy during *EVERY!* waking moment of *EVERY!* day of his *ENTIRE!* life to doing God's will?

Suddenly a coldness sweeps through Yeshua as the thought strikes him that living his life entirely for love could also cause him severe trouble — even, in extreme circumstances, his life. If large enough numbers of people were to follow him, a life lived entirely for love could upset the status quo that keeps the temple rulers, especially the Sadducees and Pharisees, in snug comfort amidst the hunger and poverty that surrounds them. The temple rulers would certainly meet any threat to the status quo with whatever force was needed — including having him nailed to a cross, the most cruel, most painful method of execution ever devised.

Yeshua shakes his head and forces the thought of dying from his mind. *If I truly am the Messiah, nothing can go wrong. If God has ordained me to do a task, and if I apply myself to that task, surely God will not allow me to fail. The creator and sustainer of all life will be with me, and nothing on earth or beyond can stand against that. No, if God has anointed me to usher in God's reign, then God will provide a way to do it.*

Though it would seem impossible for him to succeed, and dangerous for him even to try, the truth is that it actually would be impossible for him to fail. *If* he is the Messiah. *If* he does his part.

And so Yeshua chooses to trust the moment of his baptism, believe he is the Messiah, and from now on live his life accordingly. Nonetheless, he will not claim the title of Messiah, not publicly and not even to his closest friends and relatives. Claiming the title would mean nothing because people proclaiming themselves the Messiah are common throughout Palestine, and he would be just one more. More importantly, claiming the Messiahship would cause unnecessary problems because it would divide people who might otherwise hear him. Since most people have stiff ideas of what the Messiah will be, declaring his Messiahship would encourage them to expect him to fulfill their ideas, and when he disappointed them — as he certainly would — they would fall away from him without hearing him.

Furthermore, if he proclaimed himself the Messiah, the Sanhedrin could accuse and convict him of blasphemy. They would find a way to have Rome execute him.

No, if he truly is the Messiah, he knows his life must demonstrate it, but he must not claim it. If his life does demonstrate it — if he gives the people everything they need to realize a joy beyond their imaginations, regardless of their circumstances — then the people will acclaim him Messiah.

Yeshua alone will have to do the work, though. God will not do it for him. God will guide him, clear pathways for him, light the way for him, open doors for him. But Yeshua will have to lay the plans, make the decisions, choose the direction, provide the energy. God might have chosen him to be the Messiah, but it's Yeshua who will have to *BE!* the Messiah.

But how? As a Messiah, what, exactly, will he be? What, specifically, will he do?

As Yeshua weighs the possibilities, he feels strongly tempted to become exactly what most of his countrymen feel they have been promised and fully expect: a military Messiah who will destroy Rome and all of Israel's other enemies, judge the world, and establish God's eternal reign on earth with its capital in Jerusalem.

Yeshua knows he could do it. With God's full backing, he could do anything, and becoming a military leader would be the easiest choice because most of the people, especially the Zealots, expect and long for just that kind of Messiah. Great numbers of Jews would fall in behind him and fight to their death for him. As a natural leader, Yeshua could become the one to help the desperate nation overthrow the hated Roman empire.

But although Yeshua has lived his life under Rome's unrelenting dominance, and knows firsthand the revulsion of living under forced foreign sovereignty, he cannot persuade himself that God wants him to become a warrior. The God he has grown to know and trust is the God of love, not a God of force. Deciding disputes by using force is man's way, not God's way, and Yeshua knows the Messiah cannot save the world by becoming like the world. No, the Messiah must never compromise with the world. He must do everything God's way, love's way, all the way.

He recalls words from the Scriptures: "You shall worship the Lord your God and serve only him."

"*ONLY!* him, Yeshua thinks with a smile. ". . . *ALL!* your heart . . . *ALL!* your soul . . . *ALL!* your strength."

The temptation to lead militarily dissolves, but ruling out the military option begs the question: If not a military Messiah, what kind of Messiah will he be?

As he ponders the question, he notices a flat, round stone about the size of his hand, one of countless such stones that litter the wilderness floor. The stones resemble the loaves of bread his mother bakes every day in her kitchen, and suddenly Yeshua's eyes widen. He thinks of his neighbors, many of whom live every day on the threshold of starvation.

Yeshua hates seeing people go hungry, just as he knows his God does. Are the rocks a sign, an answer to a prayer? Should he use his messianic powers to bring economic justice to the world? Should he pour food on the masses until hunger is a forgotten word?

Even as he thinks it, he knows he will not do it. He could never bribe hungry people with food. That would be unthinkable. Unconscionable! Offering any kind of material reward to people, especially food to starving people, as a means to entice them to follow God would negate everything God is.

Besides, even if the Messiah did bring food to the masses, it would be food the masses came for, not the good news he brings. The people would flock to him as long as the food was there, but when the food stopped coming, so would the people.

Yeshua wants more than that for his people. He wants them to understand there is plenty of food in the world for everyone, and the only reason they are hungry is their own selfishness and foolishness. Their hunger is only a symptom of their disease; it is not the disease itself. Remove the disease from their souls and the symptoms will vanish from their bodies; remove selfishness, and hunger will cease to exist.

Yeshua wants to heal the disease, not just mask the symptoms. So no, he will not use his messianic powers to give the masses material comfort. The Messiah must give them more than that.

"It is written," he says to the wind, "'One does not live by bread alone, but by every word that comes from the mouth of God.'"

Yeshua drops to the ground and puts his head in his hands as he repeats the phrase aloud: "*EVERY!* word."

As he does so, he simultaneously senses a huge weight and a huge release.

But if he is not to be a military or economic Messiah, what is he to be? What is left? Should he be crass about it and take the easiest way out by just amazing people into following him?

He could do that, he knows. Since God would surely protect his Messiah from all harm, Yeshua could perform all sorts of dangerous stunts that the people would surely see as miracles.

He could even jump off the temple's pinnacle and survive unharmed. People would be so astounded at his signs and wonders they would have to believe he was the Messiah, and do what he said.

But Yeshua also realizes that if he performs miracles, the people will come only as long as the performances last. When the miracles end, so will the crowds, and the people will have received only a temporary diversion from their deeper-lying problems. So it would not work. It would be a temporary solution, and Yeshua wants to provide only permanent solutions.

Beside, he knows that magic-mongering is not a proper use

of God's power. Certainly the Messiah will encounter obstacles, and certainly he will have to take risks, but deliberately putting himself in danger's path and expecting God to rescue him would be a ludicrous and dangerous misuse of his power. Yeshua allows himself a slight smile as he recalls the words from Scripture and speaks them aloud:

"Again it is written: 'Do not put the Lord your God to the test.'"

But what other options are there? If he is not to be an economic or military leader, and if he won't use his power as a showman, then what is left?

Two questions abruptly appear in the void: What do I enjoy doing the most? And what do I do the best?

As soon as the questions form, so do their answers, and suddenly Yeshua knows exactly what he will do and how he will do it. What he enjoys doing most is simply being with people, and what he does best is teach. He's demonstrated his teaching abilities in the synagogues at Nazareth and Capernaum, as well as in countless private sessions with his friends. Whenever and wherever he speaks, people pay rapt attention. They listen, remember, and respond. They always have.

That's what Yeshua will do: He will simply preach and teach wherever people gather. He won't preach often, but when he does he will proclaim the theme that his cousin John learned so well and taught so pleadingly: that the reign of God has begun and people desperately need to turn away from whatever false gods they serve to dedicate whatever talents they have to serving the one true God.

Mostly, Yeshua will teach. He will teach anywhere and everywhere, in formal and informal settings, and his teaching will focus on two ideas distilled from the *Shema* and from the Ten Commandments. He will concentrate on the very basics: the need for each individual to love God and one another. They must love God by trusting him, by dedicating their lives to understanding and doing his will; and they must love their neighbors by helping them whenever they can, in whatever ways they can, by whatever means they can. If they will do that, they will experience a God-given joy they could never imagine, a fearlessness they could never envision, and a newfound freedom that will release them to do whatever they want, and do it joyously and successfully.

But nothing is without a price, and Yeshua knows the cost of following him may be steep. He frowns at the thought. He must warn his followers to expect trouble if they act on his teaching.

They won't want to hear that, but they'll have to. He will tell them and show them that a promise from God is worth incalculably more than any price they could possibly pay. Nevertheless, they must know they will pay a price.

Yeshua will teach love mostly by simply living it, and letting the results demonstrate its power. He will live his teaching so purely that his life will clearly illustrate his words. A Messiah could do that. A Messiah could live life so perfectly in cadence with God's will that anyone who looked at him would see God, and anyone who stood near him would feel God.

A Messiah could do that. Yeshua decides he will do that.

He pledges again to give his all, and withhold nothing. He has offered everything to God, and he will not turn away from the possibility that God has accepted his offer. Regardless of what the consequences may be, he will trust his baptismal experience from this moment onward. He will devote his entire life from now on to loving God and man — with *ALL!* his heart, *ALL!* his soul, *ALL!* his might. He will love without reservation, condition, judgment, or end. He will hold nothing back.

Yeshua's feet propel him toward Galilee. He joins other northbound travelers making their way along the King's Highway as it follows the Jordan River to the Sea of Galilee. At the highway's juncture with the Jezreel Valley, many travelers turn west and head toward the Mediterranean Sea fewer than fifty miles away.

Usually, Yeshua would turn with them and drop off at Nazareth, on the valley's north bank, but today he follows the highway straight to the Sea of Galilee and follows its banks around the lake to Capernaum and the fishing villages nearby. He wants to see his friends, especially Peter, Andrew, James and John. He wants to tell them everything he can of his experience — although he will stop short of claiming he is the Messiah. If he really is the Messiah, they and others will see it and name him that. Right now, he wants only to alert them that a new adventure is about to begin, and if they want to be part of it, they should start getting ready.

He has never felt so alive, so vital, so refreshed. The not-knowing is over. The decision is made. Yeshua lets out a shout as he feels the spirits of Abraham, Moses, and the prophets engulf him in joy.

3

Yeshua feels invincible as he strides into Capernaum. God wants everything Yeshua has, and Yeshua is ready to give everything. He feels as if he and God are as one. If God can't fail, neither can he. His success is assured.

Yeshua quickly finds his best friends — Peter, Andrew, John, and James — to tell them what he can of his plans. Once they are seated together on the ground, he begins.

"I will begin a new ministry soon and I will need your full-time help," he says. "It will be exciting, it will be fun, and it will be dangerous. I can't tell you any more than that now because I still have some things to do in Nazareth. I need to make plans. But when I'm ready — and it will be soon—I'll come for you. If you're with me, you'll be ready!"

"Be ready for what?" Peter asks. "Give us some details."

"To change the world," Yeshua replies quickly and firmly. "To introduce God to the world in a way the world has never seen. To teach the world the art of living joyfully regardless of circumstances. To demonstrate to the world the power and glory of a living and loving God. To. . . ."

"Whoa," John interrupts, his eyes wide. "How do you intend to do all this?"

Yeshua laughs. "Later, John."

The four are not nearly ready to accept such a brush-off so easily. Their curiosities tweaked, all four start pummeling Yeshua simultaneously with questions. What's the plan? Will we be alone or will others join us? How many? Who? When will we start? What will we do? Where? How will we work? Why?

Yeshua laughs at the onslaught. He wants to tell his friends everything, including every detail about his incredible baptism and wilderness experience. He feels as if he's about to burst, but he knows his listeners would not — could not — understand. Too much light all at once would only blind them; they would not hear him. It will be difficult enough later to make them hear him, when there is time to discuss his ideas, but that time is not now.

"Not yet," Yeshua tells them. "I've got to do some things in Nazareth before I'm ready to begin, but then I'll come back for you. You just be ready to leave when I get back. Spend your time here preparing to leave."

John rubs his chin thoughtfully. "You make some strong statements, Yeshua."

"It will be a strong ministry, John."

"You make it sound too good to be true," Andrew adds.

Yeshua smiles. "We've known each other for thirty years, Andrew. Have I ever disappointed you? Have I ever let you down? Have I ever told you I was going to do something, and then didn't do it?"

Andrew tips his head forward slightly and shows an embarrassed smile. "Actually . . . no."

"Neither will I disappoint you now."

"You sound as if you're the Messiah," Peter interjects.

Yeshua lets the question hang unanswered for a moment as he considers the question, then replies, "You decide."

With that Yeshua stands up, bids his friends good-bye, and reminds them he will return soon.

"Be ready," he says.

He returns to Nazareth, his mind racing. Who should join him in his new ministry? He will need several men to be his companions and disciples, and eventually his apostles. Peter will be his closest assistant. He, John, James, and Andrew will form his inner circle, but he will need more than just four.

Over the next weeks, Yeshua visits possible candidates throughout Galilee. He trusts his instincts to recognize the men he needs when he sees them. He chooses some men he knows personally, some he knows only by reputation, some he's never seen before. When they agree to join his ministry, he is jubilant. As he had told the others, he tells them: "Be ready when I come for you."

He continues to teach in the synagogue at Nazareth, but now with a new fire. The Nazarenes listen attentively, as they always do, but although they recognize a bold new spirit in him, they do not take him overly seriously. They don't apply his teaching to their daily lives. They've known him since he was a baby and they still see him as a child. They cannot see the man he has become. They listen, but they do not hear. They nod and talk and discuss, but they do nothing.

One day, as Yeshua is walking in the hills near his home,

some of John the Baptist's disciples arrive from the lower Jordan area with disturbing news.

"John's been arrested," one says.

Yeshua winces. He hardly has to ask the question, but he does for confirmation.

"Herod Antipas?"

"Yes. John wouldn't stop attacking Antipas over the divorce, so Herod had him thrown him into his dungeons at Machaerus, near the Dead Sea. Herod says he's going to keep John there until John agrees to stop denouncing him."

Yeshua slumps to the ground.

"John will never stop," he says blankly.

"Hardly. The more they try to silence him the louder he preaches. He preaches to the guards, to other prisoners — to anyone who's within his range. He won't let up."

"How is John dealing with being in prison?"

John's disciple lowers his eyes and swallows. "He's miserable."

Yeshua drops his head into his hands and shuts his eyes tightly as he senses the terrible anguish he knows John must be suffering. Imprisonment in a desert dungeon would be brutal punishment for anyone, but especially for John, who has spent his entire life living wild and free. Locking him away in a dungeon would be like caging a wild bird.

John's disciples, their message delivered, soon leave Yeshua alone. For a long time afterward, Yeshua remains seated motionless on the ground, deep in thought and prayer. He is fully aware of Antipas' personal loathing of John, and what has to be Antipas' gnawing frustration at his inability to control the wild man. Antipas would enjoy keeping John in pain indefinitely; of that Yeshua is certain, for Antipas can be as brutal as his father, Herod the Great, ever was. If Antipas ever concludes the only way to silence John is to kill him, he will.

Yeshua forces his thoughts away from John's dungeon cell. There is nothing he can do to save John from that, but there is much he can do to certify the validity of John's life. John started a massive movement toward God by awakening countless hearts to the understanding that all people, not just Jews, are children of God, and Yeshua indelibly identified himself with that movement when he had John baptize him. Now he must walk the path John opened and demonstrate the truth of John's teaching. He doesn't know where his new path will lead him, but he must begin walking it now, and trust God to lead him.

After awhile, Yeshua slowly stands up, brushes himself off, and heads for home. Though he has to leave Nazareth to begin his ministry, he must first tell his mother he is leaving. As her oldest living son, he has been responsible for her ever since Joseph died when Yeshua was a teenager. He has done a good job, but now his brothers and sisters are all old enough and mature enough to attend to her, so he can leave her without fear.

Yeshua finds Mary sitting in her kitchen. He already has told her all he can about his baptismal experience, and the insights he received later in the wilderness. He has warned her the day may come when he will have to leave Nazareth to follow an uncharted path. Now he must tell her that day has come. He sits beside her. After a moment, he speaks.

"I have to leave," he says quietly. "I have to begin."

Mary doesn't look up.

"I know," she says, just as quietly.

"You know?"

"John's disciples came by here today looking for you. As soon as they told me what happened to John, I knew it was time for you to begin whatever it is you have to do."

Mary raises her eyes to meet Yeshua's. When she speaks again, there is a sadness in her voice.

"I've known for many years this day would come. I've dreaded it because I know it means trouble for you."

"How did you know this day would come?"

"I think I first realized it when you astounded the rabbis with your wisdom. I also saw it coming all through your adolescence. You were a natural leader. You were better than everybody at everything, but it never spoiled you. You never made others feel inferior. You always used your gifts to help people improve themselves."

Yeshua starts to say something, but Mary raises her hand before he can speak.

"After Joseph died, I know you wanted to join one of the caravans in the valley and tour the world, and you could have — but you didn't."

"I traveled," Yeshua protests. "I went to Egypt several times."

Mary laughs. "And you always came home. If you had followed your desires, you would have stayed gone for years and made friends with every interesting person in the world. And you know it. But you didn't. You stayed home instead. You performed your duty as a widow's first-born son and took care not only of me, but your brothers and sisters as well."

"Obviously, that's what I wanted to do," Yeshua grins.

Mary glances up at him and a quick half-smile flickers across her face, but she makes no reply. Instead, they sit in silence for a moment. When Mary continues speaking, there is a pensive note in her voice.

"As soon as you returned from your baptism with John, I knew your time had come. While you talked about your experience there, you seemed lifted somehow. More focused. More directed. There was a new strength in you, a new power. And it's too big for Nazareth. You have to go."

"You don't object?"

"Of course I object. You're my son and I love you and you're walking into a terrible danger, so of course I don't want you to go. But I know you have to."

Yeshua lets a moment pass, then says quietly, "Thank you."

Mary stands up and takes his arm.

"Come with me," she says. "I have something for you."

She leads Yeshua out of the kitchen, across the patio, and into the house's main living area. Tenderly, she picks up a cloak from a table and hands it to him.

"There is a longstanding tradition among our women that we make cloaks for our sons when they begin their ministries," she says. "I made this for you."

Yeshua unfolds the garment, holds it up before him, and sees it is of the finest quality, woven in one seamless piece from top to bottom.

"It's beautiful," he says, not trying to hide his awe. "It's perfect."

"It is patterned after the tunic worn by the high priest," Mary says. "The high priest wears a seamless coat. You deserve at least that."

Yeshua hugs the cloak tightly around himself, then hugs Mary.

"I will be worthy of your trust," he whispers.

"I know," she replies.

Yeshua looks at his mother a long time before he speaks again.

"I love you," he says.

"I love you, too."

א   א   א   א

A bright sun shines from clear skies as Sabbath services begin in Nazareth. After the rituals are finished, Yeshua walks to the front of the synagogue where a rabbi hands him the sacred scroll of Scripture. Yeshua opens the scroll, quickly locates the passage he wants, and reads it aloud:

"The spirit of the Lord is upon me, because he has anointed me to bring good news to the poor. He has sent me to proclaim release to the captives and recovery of sight to the blind, to let the oppressed go free, to proclaim the year of the Lord's favor."

After he finishes, he closes the scroll and sits down, the traditional signal from a rabbi that he is about to deliver a formal, and therefore especially important, teaching. The congregation falls silent. Every person listens intently.

"Today this Scripture has been fulfilled in your hearing," Yeshua begins.

The congregation stirs in anticipation. Yeshua's teaching always leaves everyone with positive, uplifting, challenging thoughts, and they expect today to be no different. But when Yeshua continues talking, their happy moods turn to concern and puzzlement.

"No prophet is accepted by his own people," he says. "But the truth is, there were many widows in Israel in the time of

Elijah. There was a severe famine over the land, and yet Elijah wasn't sent to any of them. He was sent to a widow at Zarephath in Sidon — a non-Jewish woman. That means all people are God's children, not just Jews and not just men. We are all equal in the sight of God."

The room fills with gasps. Feet shuffle. Nervous whispers pervade the room. Then a man stands up. He hesitates before he speaks, and when he does his voice reflects serious concern.

"But Yeshua," he begins, "God chose the Jews, not the gentiles, to be his special people. God created gentiles only to be fuel for the fires of hell. You know that. That's why every one of us thanks God every day for making us Jews and not gentiles — or, nearly as bad, women. You seem to be saying God favors non-Jewish women as much as he does Jewish men. Surely you're not saying that — are you, Yeshua?"

The question hangs heavily in the air as the questioner sits down. Every person in the synagogue focuses expectantly on Yeshua. Yeshua smiles back at them.

"There also were many lepers in Israel in the time of Elisha," he continues. "But none of them was cleansed except Naaman the Syrian — a gentile."

The room erupts in fury. Men leap to their feet, shouting. The speaker points his finger straight at Yeshua.

"Blasphemer!" he roars over the din. "Exalting gentiles is blasphemy and you know it! Blasphemy! Even here, within the synagogue's walls!"

Enraged outcries slash the air until Yeshua's primary accuser, still pointing his finger at Yeshua, regains the floor and furiously shouts, "The Scriptures are very clear about what we are to do with blasphemers! We stone them to death!"

"Yes!" the crowd screams. "Stone him! Stone him now!"

As the men begin to grab for him, some of Yeshua's friends with cooler heads lunge in front of him.

"No!" they cry, stretching out their arms. "Stop! Wait! Think!"

The would-be attackers stop momentarily, but menacing anger hangs heavy in the air, an unspoken threat looking for an excuse to vent.

"Please calm down," one of Yeshua's friends pleads. "Think what you're doing. This is Yeshua! This is Joseph's son! He's been a leader in this synagogue all his life. He's been teaching all of us since he was thirteen. We all know him respect him. This is Yeshua! Let's be calm and talk."

"He is a blasphemer!" the first speaker retorts. "The Scriptures say blasphemers must be stoned to death! It is our sacred duty to stone him!"

"Yes!" the congregation erupts again. "Stone him! Now!"

"No!" shouts Yeshua's friend as he senses the congregation is becoming a mob. "You cannot even if you wanted to. Rome has suspended our Law. Only Rome can instigate capital punishment."

"We don't care!" the mob shouts. "He's a blasphemer and must be stoned!"

Yeshua's friend leaps atop a bench.

"Please!" he cries. "At least follow your own Law! It says twenty-four hours must pass between conviction and execution. You must at least follow that Law."

"He doesn't deserve the Law!" the first speaker retorts as mob control takes over. "He's a blasphemer, and he deserves to die now!"

The room explodes into a venomous shriek as the mob shoves aside Yeshua's friends and turns to grab Yeshua and secure him. But the noise of hatred quickly diminishes into a babel of confused disbelief, for Yeshua cannot be found. He has vanished. A thorough search turns up no trace of him.

Yeshua is not hiding, however. During the confusion, he had simply walked away. Now he strides out freely toward the Turan Valley and, through it, to the Sea of Galilee and Capernaum, a city where ideas of God are not frozen as they are in Nazareth.

God is for everyone, not just the Jews. All people are God's children, and all who bend their will to his are entitled to reap the joy God promises. No person — Jew or gentile, man or woman, priest or lay — is better than any other person because of the circumstances of birth. The circumstances do not matter. What matters is what a person does with those circumstances.

If Nazareth is too brittle to accept that, he will take his teaching to the world. Yeshua remains intensely aware that living and teaching love will cause him and his followers trouble. Of that there is no doubt. If members of his own synagogue tried to kill him for speaking the truth, others certainly will be likely to try.

Despite the threat, Yeshua laughs out joyfully as he strides out, firm in the belief that, regardless of what happens, he will succeed. As long as he does what God wants him to, he cannot fail. As long as he does God's will, nothing can go wrong.

4

Yeshua heads straight for the Sea of Galilee to find the brothers Peter and Andrew. He spots them sitting beside their sturdy twenty-four-foot fishing boat as they repair their nets.

"Follow me!" he shouts to them as soon as he sees them. "I'll make you fishers of men!"

Peter and Andrew shout with gladness, drop their nets and run toward Yeshua. They've been eagerly preparing for this moment ever since Yeshua returned from the wilderness and told them to get ready. They've even made arrangements with Zebedee, James' and John's father, to take over their fishing business should they need to leave in a hurry to go with Yeshua.

And why not go with Yeshua? They've known Yeshua since they were all children, and he's been their leader all along. Life was fun and exciting whenever Yeshua was around. He never hurt anybody. He seemed to love everyone, and everyone seemed to love him in return.

As soon as Yeshua's friends saw him after his wilderness experience they knew that something had changed. Something important had happened to him there, something deep. Now that he is beginning his ministry, they sense something momentous developing. They don't know what it is, but whatever it is, knowing Yeshua, it will be exciting, maybe even dangerous, and they want to be a part of it.

Yeshua knows he needs them, too — especially Peter. Peter is bullheaded and impetuous, but he's also one of the strongest and most loyal men Yeshua has ever known. Andrew is more reserved than Peter and thus he usually lives in Peter's shadow, but Yeshua knows Andrew is as loyal as Peter. Yeshua loves and needs them both.

The three quickly locate the brothers James and John, Yeshua's first cousins (their mother, Salome, is Mary's sister), at their boats nearby. James and John, who have been eagerly anticipating this moment, along with their longtime friends Peter and Andrew, are as ready as Peter and Andrew were. John and James are thunderous men, but under all their roaring, Yeshua sees a high intelligence and, especially in John, a capacity for great wisdom and deep love.

Once the five are together, Yeshua sketches a quick outline of his plan for them.

"I'll give you details later, but I'll tell you this much now: I intend to teach and preach throughout Galilee and I'll need twelve men to help me. You four will be my inner circle, but eight more men will be needed to round out the group. I've already chosen them; they're waiting for me now. The twelve of you will have three purposes. First and foremost you'll be my friends, but you'll also be my disciples, students who will learn from me. Your third role will be to become my apostles, people who will proclaim and live my teaching so others can see its truth demonstrated. I know you can only partly understand what I'm saying now, but in time it will become part of you."

"Who are the others?" asks Peter.

"Matthew for one," replies Yeshua.

"Matthew?! The tax collector?"

"The same. I take it you know him."

The four look furtively at each other.

"Yes," John says dubiously. "We know him. From afar. Purposefully from afar. He doesn't have many friends, you know."

"I know."

"Look, Yeshua, I'm not trying to tell you how to run your ministry, but won't Matthew be more trouble than he's worth? He's like all tax collectors. They take money from Jews and give it to Rome — after taking healthy cuts for themselves. They live sumptuous lives at the expense of poor people. They are hated! And Matthew is no exception! Why do you want Matthew?"

"The first time I met Matthew, he was amazed, too," Yeshua laughs. "We knew each other mostly by reputation, so he assumed I despised him as much as most other Jews do. So he was amazed when I showed up at his door unannounced and invited myself in for dinner. He was even more amazed a few hours later when he realized he was giving up his career as a tax collector to join us, even though he has only the vaguest idea of what we're about." Yeshua laughs heartily at the recollection.

None of the four asks Yeshua how he could have caused such a huge transformation in a person in such a short period of time. They know how. They've seen it. They've experienced it. But if they ask him how he does it he will answer, as he always does, with a discourse, which they can never quite fully grasp, about the power of nonjudgmental love.

They also know that Yeshua can be a hard man to turn down. His physical strength, his calm yet powerful voice, his deeply peaceful yet exciting manner, his totally accepting style, his joyous and compelling personality, his knowledge, his wisdom — they all combine to form a demeanor that can mesmerize. But, as all four have noted, the traits seem to have deepened since he returned from the wilderness.

"Who else will be with us?" John asks.

"Judas and Simon, among others," Yeshua replies.

"The Zealots?!" A chorus of four startled voices blurts in unison, their amazement over Matthew quickly turning to astonishment over Judas and Simon.

"Yes, the Zealots," Yeshua answers calmly. "I take it you know them, too."

"Of course we know them! It would be impossible not to know them! They're among the most rabid, most dangerous rebels in Galilee. You know they want nothing more than to overthrow Rome and they'll follow anyone they think stands any chance of succeeding. But Yeshua, you have no thought of overthrowing Rome, so why would you want them?"

"Activists can help us."

"Activists, yes," John says. "But loud, rabid, dangerous rebels like Zealots? Why would you want them? For that matter, why would any Zealot want you?"

"Maybe it has to do with the aura of power that Yeshua exudes," Andrew interjects. "Maybe they sense that power and realize that if anyone can bring about any significant change in the world, Yeshua can."

"Or maybe they hope to turn Yeshua's power to serve their own ends," John replies. "They might even hope to show Yeshua their ideas are better than his, make him convert to their causes, and lead them in a military mission against Rome."

Yeshua interrupts them. "Don't worry about them," he says. "They'll be fine. Judas will be our treasurer."

"Hmm," John says noncommitally. "Who else will be with us?"

"Thomas, also known as 'the twin'; Nathaniel, also known as Bartholomew; James, the son of Alpheus; Thaddeus, who also is called Lebbaeus; and Philip, from Bethsaida, the same town where Peter and Andrew live."

"I know of Thomas," John says. "He's a skeptic, almost a heckler. He won't believe anything you tell him if you don't offer irrefutable proof."

"Then I'll offer irrefutable proof," Yeshua smiles.

"I know Nathaniel," Andrew says. "He seems to be a negative sort."

Yeshua laughs aloud.

"He can be. Philip knows him especially well, and Philip has a wonderful story about the first time Nathaniel and I met. I had just returned from the wilderness and told Philip to get ready to leave home and follow me — just like I did for all of you. Philip immediately sought out Nathaniel to tell him I was planning to set out on a mission, and Nathaniel's first words were, 'Can anything good could come from Nazareth?'" Yeshua chuckles at the memory. "Philip told Nathaniel to come and see for himself, and Nathaniel did. The minute we met, I knew he was one for us. He and I talked the afternoon away, and before he left he was eager to join us. Philip reported later that Nathaniel told him, 'There is no guile in the man.'"

"I know Philip," Peter says. "We live in the same town. I

don't know him well, but he seems to be an agreeable sort." Andrew nods agreement with his brother as Yeshua smiles.

The four disciples do not recognize the names of any of the other men Yeshua has chosen, but they accompany Yeshua during the several days it takes to gather them together and lead them to Capernaum, which he tells them will be his headquarters.

Along the way Yeshua closely studies the men he has selected to lead the world into new understanding of itself. He observes everything they do, especially when they don't think he's paying any attention at all. He talks with them, listens to them, watches them. He empathizes with them so deeply that he comes to see things as they see them, hear things as they hear them, feel things as they feel them. He listens intently to their words, but equally intently to the tones in their voices, and he hears volumes they don't know they are saying. He watches their small, unconscious gestures and he perceives the profusion of information they deliver. He looks deeply into each man's heart until he knows each man better than the man knows himself.

He sees what makes them laugh, what makes them sad, what threatens them, frightens them, inspires them, angers them. He learns their strengths and weaknesses. He sees the darkness in them, darkness they try so hard to conceal, even from themselves.

He does not judge them. He loves each man deeply, honestly, thoroughly, and without condition. Thus, he shows them how they are to love each other, and all others.

He knows they will give him a chance to prove himself despite what their intellects may tell them. He knows they will trust him that much, despite their fear of trouble ahead — their fear of the unknown — that he sees in all their hearts.

"Don't worry," he smiles, and his smile alone reassures them. "I will show you how to use the power within you to conquer any fear."

א א א א

Once the men are settled in Capernaum and Yeshua sees they are beginning to become comfortable with one another, he leads them to a hillside on the northern bank of the Sea of Galilee, two miles west of Capernaum. It's a beautiful site. He selected it specifically because of its beauty and its privacy. Groves of gnarled olive trees with their silver-green leaves liberally dot the landscape. Also in abundance on the nearby hillsides are the long, broad, wind-feathered leaves of banana trees; the flat, pointed, dark green leaves of the mango trees; citrus trees of all descriptions; and plush vineyards. Like most of the rest of the country, the uncultivated ground is hard-packed and rocky, but from the spot Yeshua has selected, the knee-deep weeds glitter white gold as they wave in the morning breeze. In the distance, the Sea of Galilee reflects the blue sky.

Yeshua lets the twelve settle easily into the beauty and silence that surrounds them. He sits on a rock on the mountainside. His sitting down alerts the twelve that a formal, important teaching is about to begin. They become still.

"I've brought you here to tell you the essence of what you must understand if you are to become my apostles," Yeshua begins solemnly.

He looks slowly from face to face. A dozen men — simple men, undistinguished men, largely uneducated men, men Yeshua has chosen to lead the world into a new understanding of itself

— look back blankly. Yeshua smiles to himself. Despite the blank stares, he knows the twelve will successfully accomplish their work because he will not allow them to fail. The faces are blank now, but the day will come when they will understand him and lead the world into a new era.

Their training begins now. Yeshua will open his heart and mind to them and pour out on them the overwhelmingly good news he has to share. He knows he could say everything he has to say in one word — love. But there is too much power packed into that word for them or anyone else to comprehend, not because it is too complicated but because it is too simple. Hence, Yeshua will begin his teaching by decompressing the word. He will fully articulate its essence now, one time. He knows that even in its decompressed version, the essence of love will still be too much for his disciples to comprehend. But he will spend the rest of his life teaching it, preaching it, and, especially, living it. In time, they will understand.

Yeshua begins by describing the joy that results from living a life lavishly and wastefully for love.

"It is a happiness so great that no language can describe it, and no heart can understand it. You cannot even imagine it. But you can experience it! And those who do experience it realize a permanent, unimaginable joy that is utterly independent of anything that happens in life. It is a joy so completely self-contained that it needs nothing but itself. And nothing — not sorrow, not loss, not pain, not illness, not financial setback, not disappointment, not failure, not anything — can ever separate you from that joy."

Yeshua pauses to let his words sink in, then continues: "I am not promising you rewards in some vague future. I am telling you — and in the coming days I will show you — the joyful here-and-now consequence of a life lived fully and lavishly for love. There are no laws you must obey. There are no rules you must follow. There is only love for you to live, and a gift of priceless joy for you to accept."

"Sounds good, unbelievably good," Thomas interrupts. "But be specific."

Yeshua smiles.

"Once you realize how utterly small and ignorant you truly are in the universe, and how absolutely lost you are, you can put your entire faith in God. And when you do, this inconceivable joy permeates you. For it is only then that you can render unto God the perfect obedience it takes to do God's will as perfectly as it is done in heaven."

He reads the doubts that cloud Thomas' eyes, so he explains further: "You experience this incredible joy when you do God's will. But, you cannot do God's will as long as you are doing your own will. You'll do your own until you realize how utterly small, weak, ignorant, helpless, and lost you really are. When you actually realize that you don't know anything — you don't know who you are, where you came from, how you got here, why you're here, where here is, where you're going, or why you're going there — then you understand you are lost and alone in total darkness with no way to guide yourself out. If you turn wholly to God for guidance, and follow his guidance, you immediately touch that unassailable joy. You bring heaven to earth!"

The disciples nod thoughtfully, but Yeshua knows they don't understand. Not really. In time they will. Someday a dawn will break and they will experience the truth of what he is saying. Then they will understand. But that day is not today.

Nevertheless, he continues:

"Likewise, when you mourn for the sufferings and sorrows of others — and I mean mourn desperately, as a mother mourns the death of a child, and especially when you mourn that deeply for your own errors and your own shortcomings — then you experience the joy I'm talking about, the joy that is beyond all human understanding."

Yeshua ignores the wave of doubt he feels flow through his disciples. Instead, he suddenly grins widely, closes his eyes, and continues talking, now with laughter in his voice:

"And O! the inconceivable bliss you experience when you attain true meekness! For when you are truly meek — that is, when you comprehend how small and utterly helpless you are in the face of all that is, and when your humility banishes your pride, and when you put yourself completely under God's direction — then you discover you are in complete control of yourself. When you control yourself you control your universe, and when you control your universe you are truly great."

Yeshua looks into his disciples' eyes. "Look, you cannot successfully lead or serve others until you can control yourself, so it is crucial that you learn to control yourself, completely. But: you can only completely control yourself when you realize how truly small and utterly helpless you are compared with the universe, for it is only then that you can surrender yourself completely to the control of God. And when you place yourself under God's direction, you find you are free — free to lead others or serve others, free to use your talents to their utmost however you want to use them. Free to *live!*"

The looks on the disciples' faces tell Yeshua they still do not understand. Their intellects may grasp his words, but their hearts cannot accept them as true. Too much light is flowing in too short a time for them to absorb all the truth it bears.

Even so, Yeshua will continue talking. He wants to say it all now, one time, and then explain and expand on it for the rest of his life. He especially wants to live his words so his life can demonstrate their truth. He has a lifetime to teach his disciples, so regardless of whether they understand him now, they will in time. Yeshua closes his eyes, sits motionless for a moment, then continues.

"Listen to me," he says. "When you long to live in total harmony with God's wishes, and I mean long for it as much as a starving person longs for food or a person dying of thirst longs for water, an incredible gladness comes over you and you are satisfied."

"That's impossible," John says, not trying to hide the despair in his voice.

"You're questioning how much you really want to be in harmony with God, and you're coming up short — right?"

"Well, I do want to live in harmony with God. I am trying to follow my own direction less and follow God's direction more. The truth is, though, I don't hunger and thirst for success nearly as much as a starving person longs for food, or a person dying from thirst longs for water. And although I feel deeply for the sufferings and sorrows of others, and while I truly regret my errors, my feelings don't even compare with what a mourning mother must feel for her dead child. The truth is, Yeshua, I fall far short of your words, and as much as I'd like to think otherwise, I know I'll never measure up to them. So I don't see any reason to hope I will ever touch that unimaginable joy you keep talking about."

Yeshua nods his understanding.

"Sounds impossible, doesn't it?" he says. "Relax. You experience this joy when you truly long to live close to God, not when you achieve it. Achieving it is the destination, but your joy is not at the destination. Your joy is in the journey toward the destination. As long as you honestly long to be in harmony with God, you will naturally take the actions that will bring it about. At that point, you'll be on your journey toward total harmony, and it's there that you begin to taste the joy of which I speak."

John's despair evaporates as hope refreshes him again. "It seems so simple and obtainable when you explain it," John says. The disciples murmur their empathy as they shift with relief.

"It is simple, John," Yeshua replies softly. Then he closes his eyes again and pauses until the disciples are still again.

"And O! the unimaginable bliss that is yours when you are merciful. For it is when you are merciful that you receive mercy."

He pauses a quick moment to let the disciples register what he has said, then opens his eyes again, leans forward intently for emphasis, and explains: "It is a consistent, fundamental law of life that you get out of life whatever you put into it. If you want to receive you must give. If you want mercy you must be merciful. If you want to be forgiven you must forgive."

No one speaks, so Yeshua continues.

"Take forgiveness as an example. If you refuse to forgive someone who has wronged you, you force yourself to carry an unnecessary burden — a useless, dead weight — while the person you are refusing to forgive suffers nothing. The moment you forgive, however, that useless burden lifts from your shoulders. The more you forgive, the more burden is lifted. Forgive completely and you are forgiven completely. Then you are truly free, and your spirit soars!"

The disciples still sit quietly as they ponder his words, but their expressions tell Yeshua they still are not absorbing the importance of what he is saying.

"Look, it's a practical matter. God tells us to forgive one another without limit, just as he forgives us without limit. If you refuse to forgive someone for a wrong he has committed against you, you are willfully acting against God's wishes for you. Therefore, you are actually preventing yourself from experiencing God's forgiveness.

"How can God forgive you for missing the mark if you insist on continuing to miss the mark? You must recognize how you have strayed from God and repudiate that path before God can forgive you for taking it. You must forgive! But the instant you forgive, you are forgiven, and your soul is free.

"Take judgment as another example. Instead of judging a person, if you could realize there is a reason he does whatever he does, you are close to understanding him. But it is only when you care enough to delve into that person's mind and heart deeply enough — and without judging him — to see things as he sees them, and feel things as he feels them, that you can truly understand him. And when you do truly understand and empathize with his underlying motives, you realize there is no reason to judge him. There is no need to judge him. You are set free."

Thomas interrupts again. "I want to believe you, Yeshua, but your words seem too good to be true. They sound too simplistic. There has to be more to it than you are telling us."

"Obviously there's more," Yeshua replies. "The joy I'm talking about defies understanding, but it is obtainable. It demands a deliberate effort of the mind and the will — such as forgiving someone you don't want to forgive. It demands actively loving every person you meet."

"I have to like everybody I meet?" Thomas interjects, incredulous at the thought.

Yeshua laughs. "Of course not. You don't have to like anybody. You have to love everybody. Love them regardless of whether you like them."

Thomas thinks a moment, then begins to ask a question. But before he can ask it, Yeshua answers.

"Liking has nothing to do with loving, Thomas. Not the kind of loving I'm talking about. There are different kinds of love. There is the love that family members share among themselves. There is the passionate love involved with sexual relationships. There is the love children feel for animals. And there is the warmest, deepest love of them all: brotherly love, which is shared among the nearest and dearest of friends. All those loves share one common trait — they all involve feelings of the heart.

"But — and understand this clearly — the love I speak of concerns much more than feelings of the heart. It is an act of the will. It requires you to seek the highest good for others regardless of whether you like them, regardless of what you think of them, and regardless of what they do to you. They may hate you without cause, hurt you, laugh at you, gossip about you. And you may not like them because of it, but you must seek only their highest good in return, for this love requires you to demonstrate unconquerable benevolence and invincible good will. The result, for you, is unimaginable joy."

Yeshua sees his disciples are trying to understand, but realizing it is far too much for anyone to comprehend at once, he summarizes for them:

"To be truly merciful to someone requires you to get under that person's skin so deeply that you see and experience life the way that person sees and experiences it. That requires you to use your mind to purposefully love that person, and when you do that, you experience unfathomable mercy for yourself."

Yeshua scans his disciples' faces. Andrew is looking up at him with unabashed adoration. Peter, James, and John are listening intently to every word, fully aware they are hearing the essence of the teaching that had changed the life of John the Baptist so deeply, and wanting with all their hearts to claim that teaching for themselves. Matthew appears awestruck, as if a whole new understanding is dawning. Thomas is sitting on the ground with his knees pulled closely to his chest, arms wrapped tightly around his legs, face contorted into a frown — testimony to Yeshua that Thomas is still skeptical. The two Zealots, Judas and Simon, are mumbling disappointment to each other because Yeshua has said nothing about overthrowing Rome. Yeshua continues with a new subject:

"Listen closely," he says. "It is an unfathomable joy that comes to you when your motives are pure — when they are unmixed, unalloyed, when they all are rooted purely in God. For when that happens, you see God."

"See God?" Thomas blurts disbelievingly. His eyebrows raise as he continues to sit in a tightly wrapped ball.

Yeshua seems to ignore him and continues speaking. "You are forever fitting yourself to see God or not to see God, and when you can base all your actions on a single, pure motive — that is, when your every effort is to do the will of God" — he levels his gaze straight at Thomas — "then yes, Thomas, you see God. But it is when you know you are on the path that leads to seeing God that you experience that nameless joy."

Thomas is not persuaded. "Your words are pretty," he says. "But I need more than pretty words. You'll have to show me something. Words, theories, ideas, possibilities, promises — none of them means anything to me."

Yeshua grins broadly at Thomas. Yeshua loves skepticism. He finds cynics hard to tolerate because cynics say no to questions before they are asked, sneer at evidence before it is presented, close their minds to facts if the facts disagree with their opinions. True skeptics, though, are not like that. True skeptics say "maybe." They want to be shown, are willing to be shown, but will have to be shown. Thomas is not cynical; he is skeptical. He is not saying no; he is saying maybe. He is saying show me.

"Then I'll show you, Thomas. I'll spend the rest of my life showing you. If you'll look, you'll see the colossal power and wonder that one single life lived perfectly for love can unleash."

When Thomas fails to respond, Yeshua turns his attention back to the other disciples and moves on to a new subject.

"When you make peace among people, you are doing the work of God, and therefore will be called Godlike," he says.

"Understand that when I say 'peace' I do not mean an absence of evil or freedom from trouble. I mean the presence of everything that makes for a person's highest good.

"And also understand that I do not speak of people who merely love peace. I speak of people who make peace. A peace lover may let a dangerous situation fester for the sake of keeping the calm, but all he's really doing is postponing conflict and intensifying its force when it comes. Where peace lovers prevail over peace makers, dangerous situations ferment and explode. A peace maker, however, takes action to make peace even if that action requires a struggle."

Yeshua leans forward for emphasis and speaks with special intensity in his voice. "Listen to me!" he says. "The highest task you can perform is to produce right relationships among people. Whenever you heal breaches, bridge gulfs, or lessen strife among people in any way, you do the work of God and therefore will be called Godlike."

He leans back again, closes his eyes, and rubs his temples. He has one more thing to say and he knows his disciples aren't going to like it, but like it or not they have to hear it. They have to understand it in the depths of their souls. If they do not, all else is for nothing. He speaks slowly to emphasize his words.

"There are many people who do not want harmony with God in the world," he begins. "Some of them are afraid of God. Some think they can find a higher happiness without God. There are other reasons they exist, but be aware they do exist. So when you do the things I've been talking about, expect to find yourself in trouble. Dire trouble. Know that people who do not want harmony with God will persecute you, and sometimes they'll persecute you viciously. The more successful you are at living love, the more they will persecute you."

The disciples tense at this first hint of trouble amidst all the joy Yeshua has been promising. They want him to tell them everything will be all right, but Yeshua will not pander to their fears. They must understand and accept this.

"Look, you cannot follow me unless you are willing to suffer for me," he says. "Hear this clearly: If you want to follow

me, prepare to not only live without luxuries, but to be ostra-
cized, persecuted, maybe even killed, because powerful people
will hate you. You can expect to be accused of crimes, put on
trial, even beaten in places of worship. Some of your own family members may join those who want to kill you. You must be
prepared for such opposition, rejection, and sacrifice."

The disciples' faces accurately reflect the horror they feel,
but Yeshua only smiles in return, as he often does when matters
appear to be at their worst. He continues to speak, but now in
the calm and reassuring tones they had hoped to hear.

"Do not be concerned when those things happen, for when
they do, you are entering a society where God's will is done as
perfectly as it is in heaven. Instead of being concerned when
people revile you and persecute you, and utter all kinds of evil
against you because you are living a life of love, expect bliss.
Rejoice! Be glad! Be exceedingly glad! Your reward is great in
heaven, for that is how the prophets were treated before you."

The disciples clearly are not fully placated, so Yeshua continues.

"Look, how bad can it be if, in the midst of all the trouble,
you are experiencing unimaginable happiness and complete fearlessness?"

A titter of laughter passes among the disciples, but it is a
nervous laughter.

"I assure you," Yeshua says, "whatever happens to you will
be a light load for you to carry compared with the joy you will
experience. It will be a minuscule price to pay."

He says nothing more, but watches closely as the disciples
sit motionless, each lost in his own thoughts. They have heard
much and are trying to absorb it all, but they are overwhelmed

by its immensity. After a long moment, John breaks the silence.

"That's a lot to remember," he says. His words are released more than spoken, but they are spoken loudly enough for Yeshua to hear.

"For practical purposes, John, it is far too much to remember," Yeshua says. "So I'll simplify it for you. Just remember this and you'll know everything I have to teach: When you make loving God and loving people the point of your life, everything else takes care of itself. Put another way, whenever you seek out what it is that God wants you to do, and you do it, and whenever you do whatever you can to make life better for those people whose paths cross yours, then you fulfill all the demands that God makes on you. Do just those two things — love God and love your neighbor — and you will be ridiculously happy, completely fearless, and, yes, constantly in trouble."

5

Yeshua is on the streets of Capernaum early the next morning to begin his public ministry. He sees a group of fishermen talking and he joins them. Soon, by sheer force of personality, he is leading the conversation. He steers it to God. He speaks of God in ways they've never heard, as a good father who loves all his children and wants to be a part of their lives, to commune with them, help them. He speaks of a joy beyond their understanding that living in harmony with God will produce. He speaks with a joy that radiates from his whole being.

The fishermen are mesmerized, both by the teacher and his teaching. Long after he leaves them, they remain locked in deep conversation about the astonishing man from Nazareth.

Yeshua spends the day talking to people wherever they gather — on fishing docks, in fields, on the roadside, beside the Sea of Galilee. He does not waste his time trying to prove the existence of God because he knows full well it is impossible to prove God's existence — or, for that matter, God's nonexistence.

But he knows that anyone who wants to experience God can do so, and he focuses on that. He talks of a spiritual father who loves his children, wants the best for them, and provides for all their needs when they turn away from whatever false gods they worship — money, power, status, security, prestige — and believe the astoundingly good news Yeshua brings.

"That does not mean you can merely give intellectual assent to the idea," he cautions. "It means that you must base everything you do, every decision you make, on the certain knowledge that the God of all creation is with you. The result for you will be unimaginable joy in the here-and-now, regardless of your situation."

Mostly, though, Yeshua loves the people he meets simply and wholeheartedly. He doesn't care if they are Jew or gentile, rich or poor, male or female, old or young. He doesn't care what their religion is. He loves them all as they are, genuinely and unconditionally. He loves them so deeply that he sees life as they see it and thereby empathizes with what they feel. He looks beyond the facades they build to hide behind, and he sees the people as they really are. He sees them more clearly than they see themselves.

The people feel naked in front of him, but they are not ashamed. They sense he sees their ugliest secrets and knows their most depraved thoughts, yet none of it matters to him. He sees, but he does not judge. He loves them for what they are, whatever they are, and they know it.

The people he meets tell others of this astounding teacher, and the others respond by seeking out Yeshua to see and hear for themselves. Then they tell others, who tell others, who tell others. . . .

Soon people from all around are flocking to see and hear him. There are fishermen, farmers, tax collectors, craftsmen, merchants, and they include Jews and non-Jews, rich and poor, men and women. Women respond especially joyfully to his teaching that all people are equal in the sight of God. No Jewish leader has ever recognized them as equals before.

The more the crowds hear, the more they want to hear, and the crowds grow rapidly. Soon, throngs of people are coming to hear him wherever he goes. Once the crowds press so hard on him while he is teaching by the lakeside that he has to take a boat offshore and teach from the water.

It is an idyllic time, a time of success upon success, a time when dreams seem to come true for everyone. Wherever he goes, things change — attitudes change. People find it exciting and fun just to be near him, and the crowds that surround him are always joyous. In his presence, his laughing and joyous presence, people find it hard to do anything but love one another.

He touches a sick person and the love that flows through him is so genuine, so pure, so powerful, that it by itself provides the encouragement, strength and confidence the person needs to heal. Yeshua's touch alone awakens sick people from the threshold of death.

After one such experience, Yeshua is approached by one of John the Baptist's disciples.

"How is John?" Yeshua immediately asks.

"He's like a caged wild animal. He's dying a slow death, but he hasn't stopped rebuking Herod Antipas and his wife."

A sad, faint smile touches Yeshua's face. "I didn't expect otherwise. Did John send you here or did you come on your own?"

"John sent me. Soon after he baptized you he started implying to us that you might be the Messiah. He never said you were; he just hinted you might be. Soon after that, he was taken to the dungeon. He's had a lot of time alone there to think about it, and now he believes with all his heart you are the Messiah. He hopes he's right, but more than anything he wants confirmation of that hope. So he sent me here to ask you bluntly: Are you the Messiah?"

Yeshua doesn't hesitate before he answers.

"Tell John it doesn't matter what I say. It matters only what I do. If I do the work of the Messiah, I am the Messiah. If I do not do the work of the Messiah, I am not the Messiah. So don't tell John what I say. Tell him instead what you see happening here. The lame are walking. Sick people are being made well. Broken people are being made whole again. Dead spirits are being revived. Poor people are receiving and responding to the good news. John can decide for himself if I am the Messiah."

When the next morning arrives, Yeshua sends John's disciple on his way, then resumes his teaching and preaching. Several weeks pass and he hears nothing more. But one day he looks out over the crowds and sees John's disciple returning. The disciple walks slowly, almost shuffles, and appears slightly slumped over.

As he approaches Yeshua, Yeshua can read the sadness in his heart.

"John's dead, isn't he?" Yeshua asks, expressionless.

"Yes. Antipas had him beheaded."

Yeshua turns his head away in pain as the disciple continues.

"It came during a birthday celebration for Antipas at the fortress at Machaerus, where John was being held. Antipas' step-daughter danced for the celebration. When she finished, Herod was so impressed that he offered to give her anything she wanted, up to half of his kingdom. She conferred with her mother — Antipas' new wife, the one John rebuked — about what she should ask for. When she returned she told Antipas she wanted John's head on a silver platter. Antipas could have refused, of course, but he didn't want to back down from a public promise. Beside, it gave him the excuse he needed to get rid of John without starting a riot. So he sent the guards out immediately, and they returned in less than an hour with John's head — on a silver platter, as requested."

Yeshua feels ill. John was his first cousin, his best student — his best friend. John had fearlessly opened a path into the night where there had been none, enabling Yeshua to bring the good news of God to all people. But John was incapable of seeing evil without rebuking it, and that trait alone cost him his life.

"I want to be alone for a while," Yeshua tells Peter. He walks into some nearby hills that overlook the River Jordan, and spends the rest of the night alone, in quiet, deep contemplation and prayer.

The next morning, he is back, more eager than ever to complete his mission, regardless of the cost. He begins to teach on a hillside near Tabatha. Throngs of people have walked long distances to be near him, but as time to eat approaches, it becomes apparent there is not nearly enough food to feed everyone. Yeshua's disciples barely have enough fish and bread to feed themselves, much less the crowd that surrounds them.

They began to worry.

"If we can't feed them, they'll riot," Peter tells Yeshua. "What can we do?"

Yeshua smiles his out-of-place smile. "Don't worry," he says. "Food will appear when it is needed."

Then he speaks to the crowds. He speaks of simple love, of the need for each person to put others ahead of himself, of the necessity of making certain the other person has what he needs before you take what you want. He assures them there is always enough of everything for everybody when people treat one another as they themselves want to be treated. He closes by announcing it is time eat and asks everyone to demonstrate that love by sharing whatever they have with those around them so that everyone will have enough.

As he sits down with his disciples, he looks at Peter and says, "Do you really think this many people would walk this far, to a remote hillside far away from civilization, without planning for food?"

'Well, no. . . .'

"Of course not! Most of them would bring food as a matter of routine. The problem is not a lack of food. The problem is a hoarding of food by selfish, frightened people, people who fear that if they share what they have with others they won't have enough for themselves."

Yeshua looks out to the crowds around him. "But now that these people understand something about love, they'll all share, and everyone will eat."

Yeshua reaches for a pickled fish as the astonished disciples look to the crowd. People are reaching inside their cloaks to produce fish and loaves of bread. Most have plenty of food to share, which they do, and everyone eats his fill. When the feast ends, everyone is well-fed, happy, and there is food left over.

"If all of us would consider everyone else's problems as our own — as you saw happen today — we would overcome all problems," Yeshua tells his disciples. He grins widely. "If we did, we'd be working miracles all the time."

A few days later, Yeshua is teaching gentiles in Galilee east of the Jordan when the same problem occurs. Many people have walked miles to hear Yeshua teach, but time comes to eat and there is no food apparent. So, just as he did among the Jews, Yeshua leads his listeners into making the decision to share, and once again there is plenty of food for everyone with some left over. A miracle, many say. But Yeshua insists otherwise.

"Our father gives us everything we need, physically as well as spiritually and mentally," he tells his disciples when the day has ended. "Food is an example. Our father puts plenty of food into the world for everyone, but he leaves its distribution up to us. When people start fearing they won't have enough for themselves they begin hoarding it. Sharing ends then, and hunger enters the world. Eliminate fear and hunger vanishes."

צ צ צ צ

Yeshua and some of his disciples are relaxing on the Sea of Galilee in Peter's wooden fishing boat when the dry, cool winds from the mountains swoop down on the warm, moist air over the lake and create a sudden, violent storm. Harsh winds churn the lake's normally placid waters into angry, crashing waves. Blinding rain slashes into the disciples' eyes as they pit all their strength against the elements. But the winds are too strong, the rain too blinding, the waves too heavy. They can't make any headway; it's all they can do just to keep the boat from capsizing.

The storm increases and whips them even harder. Waves

pound down on them and threaten to swamp the boat. As the men feel themselves losing control, they begin to panic and thrash their oars wildly in a desperate attempt to stay afloat.

All the time, Yeshua sits in the boat's bow. He had been sleeping, but now he is awake and alert and watching closely. As his disciples begin to panic, he shouts to them over the tumult, "God is with us. There's nothing to fear. Do what you're trained to do and we'll be fine."

Yeshua howls with laughter as another wave pounds down on the boat, and his fearlessness dispels the disciples' panic. Each disciple knows from long experience what must be done to keep the boat afloat and each knows his individual part in it. With their composure returning now, each man stops his wild thrashing and begins doing what he knows he must do. Soon the boat is heading into the waves again, and the storm passes without causing further harm.

Later, as the disciples row easily toward shore, John has a question. "You said God was with us and therefore we'd be fine — which we are. Does that mean God prevented us from sinking and saved our lives?"

"No, it means you're fine," Yeshua answers. "With God, regardless of what happens, you're fine."

Yeshua reads the puzzlement on John's face, so he explains. "Death is not evil. Death is merely the other side of birth. You cannot have one without the other, just as you cannot have a top without a bottom or a left without a right. They are necessary parts of the same thing. So yes, of course, we all might have died. We put ourselves in the way of nature and the storm could have sunk us. But even if we had all died, everything would have been fine."

John frowns as he contemplates his teacher's words. Yeshua goes back to sleep in the bow of the boat.

צ צ צ צ

As the stories of Yeshua's exploits spread (and become more embellished with every retelling of them) many people begin calling Yeshua a miracle worker. But Yeshua, who decided in the wilderness he would not use miracles to attract followers, adamantly rejects the label.

"You or anyone else can produce the same results I do," he tells his disciples. "You can produce even more impressive results than you have seen me produce. All you have to do is accept my teaching about love as absolute, and boldly act on that knowledge. When you do, these so-called 'miracles' will happen for you."

The disciples try to take it in and think they do, but Yeshua knows they do not. It is still too much light in too short a time for them to fully absorb. Too much light at once is blinding, so each disciple sees only what he can allow in. Everything else is merely words.

But Yeshua won't stop to placate his disciples. The subject of miracles is important to him. While he was in the wilderness, he rejected the temptation to harvest believers by working miracles. Now he is determined to do whatever is necessary to prevent his so-called miracles from interfering with his teaching.

"Understand this clearly," he tells the disciples. "You do not have to believe in miracles to reap the benefits of my teaching. Nor should you believe in miracles. Any faith that depends on miracles is false, and we will leave any region if it becomes apparent that people are responding to my 'miracles' instead of my teaching. Remember this: What people call miracles are merely signs that God is doing what God said God would do. They in themselves are not important. Love is the only thing that is important. Nothing else matters. Nothing!"

Yeshua's words help the disciples focus on his teaching, but no one can stop the masses from murmuring among themselves about miracles that Yeshua works.

And the "miracles" continue.

While walking along a road with his disciples, he chances upon a man who is raving incoherently to himself as he stumbles along. As soon as the man sees Yeshua walking with his disciples, he suddenly cries out excitedly:

"What do we have to do with you, Yeshua? Have you come to destroy us? I know who you are! You are the Holy One of God!"

"Do not say that!" Yeshua replies, instantly and sharply. "Do not start that rumor!"

"I will not be silenced!" the man shouts back, wildfire in his eyes. "You're the Messiah! You're the Messiah! You're the Messiah!"

Yeshua walks directly up to the man until their faces are inches apart. He locks eyes with him and orders in a loud, bold, authoritative voice, "Be quiet and come out of him!"

With a loud cry the man falls to the ground in convulsions. Yeshua steps back and watches. After a few moments, the man becomes still and silent. Yeshua continues to watch. More moments pass. Then the man slowly rises to his feet again. He is quiet now, almost shy, and appears to be confused, stunned, embarrassed. He looks up at Yeshua.

"Thank you, sir," he murmurs. Yeshua smiles as the man quickly melts into the crowd and disappears.

As Yeshua returns to his walk, those who witnessed the event — especially the man's friends who saw what happened — begin to wonder even more what special powers Yeshua must have that allows him to do such things. None of them mentions the word Messiah in Yeshua's presence. Yeshua himself never broaches the subject.

Still, Yeshua is as caught up as anyone in the euphoria over the stunning success he is experiencing. He is only a few months into his ministry and already multitudes of people are responding. He is doing what he loves to do and what he does well, and he is dedicating the results to God, which is to say he is doing the will of God. And God seems to be accepting his efforts. For that, Yeshua constantly breathes prayers of gratitude and thankfulness.

However, even in his euphoria, Yeshua remains aware that his fame could become as dangerous to him as his successes have been exhilarating. With every passing day he becomes more and more aware that the reports of his fame, plus what almost certainly are greatly exaggerated reports of his work, must have reached Jerusalem by now. And since Jerusalem is home of the temple rulers, the rulers surely must at least be apprehensive. At some point, they will have to send emissaries to Galilee to investigate him, and when they arrive they will certainly see him and his teaching as a threat to their cherished way of life, their social status, their power, their sources of money, their religion — their lives. Most likely they will respond by doing whatever is necessary to silence him, even if that means having him killed. He realized while he was in the wilderness that a life lived fully and lavishly for love would be full of risks and dangers, but he cannot fathom what dangers will present themselves or when they will begin. He prays for the wisdom and strength he will need to face whatever form the dangers assume when they come.

He does not have to wait long. It begins subtly one day while he is teaching inside a house in Capernaum. Swarms of people have come to see and hear him, and those who cannot fit into the house press around the doors and windows to catch a glimpse of him, perhaps even to touch him. One is a paralytic whose four friends have brought him to Yeshua, fervently believing that if Yeshua will only touch him, he will be healed.

The men cannot get their friend through the throng that surrounds the house, so they hoist him to the roof, open a hatch, lower him into the room on a mat, and place him directly in front of Yeshua. When Yeshua sees the faith the man and his friends have, he is overcome and says simply, "My son, everything you have ever done to hinder the work of God in the world is forgiven."

Immediately, a small knot of men inside the house begin to carp loudly among themselves.

"You can't forgive sins!" one of the men shouts at Yeshua. "Only God can forgive sins, yet you forgive this man's sins. That's clearly blasphemy! And the Scriptures say the penalty for blasphemy is death by stoning. Why shouldn't you be stoned to death, Yeshua?"

Yeshua drops his hands to his side. For a long moment, he stands still and silently as he looks deeply into the man's eyes, whom he recognizes as a Pharisee. *So this is how they'll attack me,* he thinks. *These Pharisees want to trap me by entangling me in their endless rules and regulations, and if they succeed they'll have the excuse they need to have me killed.*

"Well?" The Pharisee hurls his words at Yeshua. "Speak to

us. Everyone here heard you tell this crippled man his sins are forgiven, but since only God can forgive sins, you are guilty of blasphemy. It's as simple as that. And since the Scriptures clearly say blasphemy must be punished by death, I want to know why you think you should live."

Yeshua takes a deep breath and lets it out slowly. "Why do you raise such questions in your hearts?" he finally asks, a touch of weariness born of exasperation in his voice. "Why won't you understand?"

The Pharisee says nothing. Yeshua continues. "Which is easier to say to this man: 'You are forgiven for failing God,' or 'Stand up and take your mat and walk'?"

The Pharisee freezes. Something in Yeshua's voice, in his eyes, in his manner, tells the Pharisee he's missed something important. He feels vulnerable, but doesn't know why. He says nothing, fearing he might make matters worse.

Yeshua smiles easily, almost lovingly, into the Pharisee's eyes before he continues.

"You teach that illness is caused by failure to obey God, and since only God can forgive such a failure, only God can heal illnesses. Is that correct?"

The Pharisee nods slightly, dubiously.

"We all know it is easy to say, 'Your sins are forgiven,'" Yeshua continues, "for whether or not the sins are forgiven could not be proven. But, if I were to tell this man to get up and walk, and he got up and walked, then, by your own teaching, it would have to be because God had forgiven his sins. Is that correct?"

The Pharisee stares back at Yeshua and nods his head slightly, but he says nothing. Yeshua lets a moment pass. Then, his eyes still locked on the Pharisee, he finishes: "So that you may know the son of man has authority on earth to forgive people who fail God" — now he turns back to the paralytic, smiles reassuringly at him, touches his forehead, lowers his voice, and says with genuine love and kindness in each word — "I say to you, stand up, take up your mat, and go home."

The man leaps to his feet and, as the room explodes into shouts of joyous surprise, bolts for the door, crying out loudly and praising God as he runs.

Without another word, the Pharisees angrily grab up their belongings and storm from the house. Yeshua had entangled them in their own teachings and left them no way out.

"He also just declared himself the Messiah — did you hear that?" one of the Pharisees mutters as they leave. "He called himself the son of man. That's a title from Scripture that has been used occasionally, but always obliquely, in reference to the coming Messiah. Yeshua referred to himself as the son of man, but the meaning is so vague in the Scriptures that we cannot openly accuse him of calling himself the Messiah, although we all know that is exactly what he did. He knows it, too. He deliberately implied that impression."

As Yeshua watches the Pharisees storm away, he hears the word "miracle" being bandied about.

"No!" he almost barks. "Just because something appears to be beyond nature does not mean *is* beyond nature. It might just mean you don't understand nature. A lot happens that you cannot explain, but that does not mean it is a miracle."

6

The Pharisees do not wait long before they strike again. They find Yeshua walking easily toward the Sea of Galilee, teaching his disciples and others who follow them as they stroll in the morning sun. The Pharisees fall into step with the crowd so they can observe Yeshua and look for reasons to discredit him.

On the way to the lake they pass the home of Matthew, the despised tax collector whom Yeshua made a disciple. Matthew invites Yeshua and the other disciples to join him in his home for dinner.

Yeshua accepts the invitation, but as soon as they sit down, the Pharisees, who have remained outside the house, pull some of Yeshua's disciples aside and attack.

"Those people Yeshua is sitting with are people of the land," a Pharisee snarls. "They are common people, people who are too ignorant or too stupid to follow the Scriptures, and are therefore unclean. Yeshua knows that, yet he sits with them. It's unconscionable!"

The disciples blanche. Based on the Pharisees' interpretation of Scriptures, orthodox Jews are forbidden to have any contact with ritually unclean people unless it is absolutely necessary. Clean people do everything they can to avoid doing business with any people of the land. Clean people would never travel with them, or even talk unnecessarily with them. And above all, no strict keeper of scriptural Law would ever show hospitality to or accept hospitality from a person of the land.

"Yeshua knows these people are unclean, and yet he openly defies convention by sitting with them," the Pharisee nearly howls. "How can you men possibly associate with him, much less defend him?"

Before the disciples can answer, Yeshua appears in the doorway. He overheard the Pharisees' grumblings and he is ready with an answer.

"People who are healthy do not need a physician," he says. "Only people who are ill need physicians. Likewise, I am not here to save people who live harmoniously with God, but those who have removed themselves from God's family and are therefore sick in their souls. They are the ones who need me, and they are the ones I will serve."

His answer infuriates the Pharisees.

"But all our disciples fast," one protests. "Even the disciples of John the Baptist fast. Why don't your disciples fast?"

Yeshua sighs. "They do fast," he says wearily. "They fast. I fast. We all fast. We all know fasting is good. Fasting focuses a person's life, and helps him realize he can master his life. Also, purposefully doing without a gift from God for a short time increases our appreciation of that gift. So yes, we all fast.

"But, we do not fast according to your rules. Your idea of

fasting, like most everything else you do, is built on a foundation of legalisms and hypocrisy. You fast only to obey the Law so others will see how holy you are. To you, love is irrelevant. Even God is irrelevant to you!"

The Pharisees are aghast at the insult, but Yeshua ignores them and continues speaking, his voice becoming quieter and more measured now. He is thankful for the opportunity to teach another important lesson.

"I'm sure you know that the temple rabbis have ruled that all people attending the bridegroom during his wedding celebration are relieved from any religious observances that may lessen their joy or the joy of the bridegroom," he says. "As long as the bridegroom is with the attendants, therefore, they cannot fast. Only when the bridegroom leaves them and the celebration is over can they fast again."

When the Pharisees say nothing, Yeshua continues. "You do not use new cloth to mend an old garment, for you know the strong new cloth would shrink and tear the brittle old cloth and make the problem worse than before. Neither do you pour new wine into old wineskins, for the new wine will expand and burst the brittle old wineskin, destroying both."

Now Yeshua levels his glare at his accusers and speaks his words deliberately and slowly so the Pharisees cannot possibly misunderstand him.

"Likewise, my teachings will not fit into your brittle old molds. Your molds are part of the old legalism, and they cannot possibly contain the new teaching."

The Pharisees feel insulted, but are left speechless. They turn away abruptly and storm from the house. Yeshua returns to the dinner party, but he knows the Pharisees will only regroup and return. He thinks, *Strike and withdraw, strike and withdraw. How appropriate was John's description of them as a "brood of vipers."*

צ צ צ צ

It is on a Sabbath when the Pharisees strike again. As Yeshua and his disciples head for the synagogue in Capernaum, the Pharisees follow closely, looking for any breach of the Law or the scribes' regulations that they can use to discredit him.

They find it even before they get to the synagogue. As they walk through a grainfield, some of the disciples break off ears of grain, rub them in their hands, and eat them.

On most days, the practice is perfectly legal and acceptable; travelers are allowed to eat from any field as long as they do not use a sickle or other mechanical means to cut and harvest. On a Sabbath, however, all work is forbidden, and the scribes' thirty-nine classifications of work include reaping, winnowing, threshing, and preparing a meal.

"Your disciples are breaking all four of those rules," one of the Pharisees yells excitedly at Yeshua. "You can't deny they are breaking the Law. What are you going to do about it?"

"Nothing," Yeshua replies as the disciples keep eating.

"Nothing? What do you mean nothing? Why not?" the horrified Pharisees all demand at once.

"Don't you know your own Scriptures?" Yeshua asks. "Haven't you read what King David did when he became hungry during the time Abiathar was high priest? He entered the House of God and ate the consecrated bread! Not only that, he gave some of the bread to his companions so they could eat, too. It was absurd for them to be hungry in the presence of plenty."

The Pharisees remain surly, but otherwise quiet.

"Don't you see?" Yeshua asks in exasperation. "God made the Sabbath for the benefit of man. He did not make man for the benefit of the Sabbath!"

Yeshua does not wait to gauge if he has made any impact on the Pharisees. He knows he has not. Their ears and eyes, like their minds and hearts, are closed to anything that does not fit within their rigid rules. They do not listen, so they do not hear. Instead of wasting any more time with them, Yeshua and his disciples proceed on toward the synagogue.

The Pharisees remain close behind them, eager to get to the synagogue because that will be the perfect place to observe Yeshua. If they can catch him in a breach inside the synagogue, they will have him exactly where they want him. Synagogues are arms of the temple and, therefore, many people will be present who believe as the Pharisees do. They will make excellent, willing witnesses before the Sanhedrin.

As soon as the Pharisees enter the Galilean synagogue, they are recognized as honored guests. They are offered the synagogue's best seats on the front row, which they accept with a flourish. They feel that as Jerusalem Pharisees they deserve the honor. Moreover, here they can observe Yeshua closely. Here, in this building, they rest secure in the knowledge that Yeshua is as good as dead if he gives them any cause whatever.

Yeshua gives them cause very soon. Indeed, he gives them the best opportunity they've ever had to accuse him.

As Yeshua begins teaching, he notices a man in the congregation whose hand is withered. The Pharisees notice him too, and they wait to see if Yeshua will attempt to heal him. If he does, they can accuse him of blasphemy, for the Law specifically prohibits work on the Sabbath and the scribes have labeled most forms of healing as work. The scribes are abundantly clear about that and have developed numerous rules to cover every conceivable situation. Only if a person's life is threatened can any medical attention be given. A woman giving birth can be helped, but a man with a broken leg cannot be. A cut may be bound to stop the bleeding, but no ointment may be applied to the wound to help it heal. The strict Pharisee will not even defend his life on the Sabbath should he be physically attacked. A withered hand, therefore, plainly does not qualify for legal healing on the Sabbath.

But when Yeshua sees the withered hand, he does not hesitate to act. He immediately calls the man to come forward and stand where everyone can see him. The man does as he is bid, as the Pharisees lean in intently to watch.

Yeshua turns to the Pharisees and asks, "Is it lawful to do good or to do evil on the Sabbath?"

The Pharisees freeze. They realize Yeshua once more has hooked them on the horns of a dilemma. If they speak at all they will have to admit it is right to do good on the Sabbath, and restoring a man's withered hand does seem a good thing to do. Further, if pressed, they also will have to admit it would be evil not to do good should the occasion present itself, so leaving a man in wretchedness when it is possible to help him is surely evil.

When Yeshua sees the Pharisees are not going to answer him, he drives his point home. "Is it lawful to save a life or take a life?" he asks, bluntly and loudly.

This one really stings them. Yeshua is comparing himself with them and they know it. There is no way they can win.

They have not come to the synagogue to worship God, but to find a way to kill Yeshua, whereas Yeshua has come to teach and heal. In their hearts they know it is better to help a person live than to plan a person's death. But, since the Pharisees follow their rules more than their hearts, the point is quickly lost.

"The Law plainly says healing is work, and work is forbidden on the Sabbath," a Pharisee points out. "Therefore, if you heal anyone here today, you are breaking the Law and must be punished. It is as simple and as irrefutable as that."

A wave of anger sweeps over Yeshua. The Pharisees' self-imposed blindness, and especially their blatant hypocrisy, infuriate him. He abhors hypocrisy. He reserves his harshest words for hypocrites because they only pretend to follow God. In reality they follow their own desires. They are liars. They lie to each other and to themselves. They place a false face on the religion they pretend to love, and when others see that false face, they are pushed away from God all together. The Pharisees include some sincere, good men, albeit misguided men, among their numbers. But many of them, perhaps most of them, are among the worst hypocrites in Palestine. Those are the men who stand before Yeshua now, accusing him. They mock the very God they say they love.

Yeshua does not address the Pharisee's claim. Instead, he focuses his attention on the man with the withered hand, who stands nervously between Yeshua and the closely watching line of Pharisees. Yeshua sees the man is a stonemason who must have his hands to work, but his hand is paralyzed as the result of an illness.

"Stretch out your hand," Yeshua tells the man.

As he does, Yeshua reaches out for it, folds it inside his own hands, and holds it close to his chest. He speaks to the man in tones so low and personal that only the man can hear him. As the man looks up to into Yeshua's eyes, he senses that Yeshua knows him better than he knows himself, yet loves him without condition despite all his many shortcomings. He feels enmeshed inside an aura of love that is stronger than anything he has ever experienced. A warm, loving, encompassing energy flows through Yeshua, through his hands, through the man's crippled hand. The hand moves.

Yeshua immediately steps back and looks kindly at him. "You are healed," he says.

The man hesitates, then slowly holds out his hand. Everyone there sees it move again.

The Pharisees leap to their feet, more furious than ever because they are helpless to do anything about this magic. They don't even wait to see what happens next. They simply stalk out of the synagogue and out of sight.

As Yeshua watches the Pharisees storm away, he knows he has won the skirmish, but it brings him no joy. It was only a skirmish; it was not the war. There will be other skirmishes. The Pharisees have not retreated in defeat; they have only withdrawn to regroup. They will be back, filled with renewed resolution and armed with better traps.

Once the Pharises are gone, a man asks Yeshua: "His hand was witheed. Now it isn't and you say that's not a miracle? Well, if it's not a miracle, what is it"

This time Yeshua only grins, widely. "Just God doing what he said he would," he replies.

צ צ צ צ

"This time Yeshua has overstepped all boundaries," the Pharisees' leader fumes as they storm away from the synagogue. "He defiantly performs work on the Sabbath — and he does it openly inside the synagogue. He mocks our rules and regulations. Now we must stop him! If we don't stop him soon, it will only be a matter of time before all the rabble will be believing him and flocking to him."

By the time they are settled down for the night they have reached full agreement that Yeshua must not merely be stopped, but stopped permanently. He has gone too far to be merely silenced and punished.

"He must die," their leader says. "There is no other choice, and there is no going back."

"But how?" another replies. "We seem powerless to trap Yeshua. Face the facts: Like it or not, he has easily thwarted every one of our traps. He's even turned our traps against us and entangled us in our own words."

Silence falls over the group as each member realizes he is right. None of them has any new ideas to trip him up — none that they would dare use, anyway — and they have nothing to tell the Sanhedrin that would stand up against cross-examination in court. They certainly have nothing that could be converted into a charge of insurrection.

At nearly midnight, one of the Pharisees says quietly, "We could talk with the Herodians."

"The Herodians?" several surprised voices ask at once. A palpable shiver moves through the group like a shadow.

"Yes, the Herodians," the Pharisee says defensively. "King Herod is a puppet of Rome, so he has the authority to apply capital punishment in Galilee any time he wants to. If we could convince the Herodians that Yeshua is a threat to Herod — whom they exist to support — they would either haul him before the king to be beheaded or, more likely, they'd do it themselves."

"But — the Herodians," another man stammers, still not believing the name had even come up. "Herodians do not observe ritual holiness, you know that. They're unclean. If we have any dealings with them, we'll become as unclean as they are."

"That is true," says the first. "But we can be cleansed later. Unless, of course, you have a better idea?"

"No, but. . . ." The complainer sinks into silence. He hates the idea of dealing with a Herodian, but he has no better idea.

"Why would the Herodians help us?" another asks.

"Because there's already bad blood between Herod and Yeshua," the first answers quickly, his optimism rising as a plan begins to solidify in his mind.

"Herod Antipas had John the Baptist beheaded because John refused to quit railing against him. Wouldn't Herod like to know Yeshua is John's first cousin? And is preaching the same thing John was?"

His voice trails off in thought, then suddenly picks up with a new spark.

"Also, I think it can be proven — to Antipas' satisfaction anyway — that Yeshua was one of those children who escaped Bethlehem when Antipas' father, Herod the Great, had all the male children there killed to prevent a king from growing up. Remember? Wouldn't Antipas be interested to know that Yeshua escaped, and today multitudes of people are worshiping him as if he were their king?"

The Pharisees talk into the night. No one wants to deal

with the Herodians, but, as dawn approaches, no one has offered a better idea, and they admit they have no other choice if Yeshua is to die. Even fully believing they will become unclean themselves, the Pharisees agree to approach the Herodians.

7

The Pharisees leave Yeshua alone while they gingerly begin establishing contact with the Herodians. No one harasses him as he walks and teaches in the streets, sits and teaches in the synagogues, or preaches in the fields and beside the waters. They simply vanish from his view.

Yeshua knows they are planning a new attack, but he does not know what it will be, where it will come from, or when it will come. All he knows for certain is that it is coming. The Pharisees will not back down. They cannot back down — not if they are to protect their treasured standard of living.

Yeshua takes advantage of their withdrawal. It gives him time to teach, preach, and demonstrate unhindered by the hecklings and carpings of closed-minded hypocrites.

He sets up on the shores of the Sea of Galilee to teach, preach, and heal. The response is immediate and overwhelming. His fame has spread, and people from all around flock to hear him. Most come from Galilee, but substantial numbers also pour in from Jerusalem and other parts of Judea to the south; from the gentile region around Tyre and Sidon on the Great Sea to the northwest; and from the gentile country across the Sea of Galilee to its east. They come to hear him teach and see him heal. Many come to be healed. Others come because they have experienced his powerful presence before and they want to experience more. They come to see miracles. They come out of curiosity. They come because of his celebrity. But they come. And they listen. And many hear.

The only major distraction to Yeshua during these idyllic days is that some of the same raving people who had named Yeshua the Messiah during the early days of his ministry still insist on pestering him. They thought he was the Messiah in the early days and they still think so, and they will not be silenced. They throw themselves down in front of him as he tries to teach, and they constantly cry out, "You are the son of God!"

Yeshua repeatedly demands that they not call him that and that they not worship him. "I am not good," he tells them. "Only God is good. By focusing your attention on who I am, you are missing the whole point of my teaching — the whole point of your lives!"

His pleadings, however, only make them cry out and demonstrate all the more.

Yeshua refuses to let the unwanted recognition slow his mission. He senses he has limited time before the Pharisees return, so he does everything he can to make the most of every opportunity. He uses every teaching device he knows. He keeps his teaching simple and direct so that every word counts. He often repeats himself for emphasis. His favorite tool is the parable because it illustrates a single religious truth in an unforgettable way, but he also acts out prophetic passages, using whatever is at hand to illustrate his teaching. He often draws word pictures based on his listeners' lives so they will understand and remember what he says. He teaches in paradoxes that shock his listeners' minds to alertness.

"The last will be first and the first will be last," he says.

"Whoever saves his life will lose it, and whoever loses his life for my sake, and for the sake of the good news I bring, will save it."

His style mesmerizes his listeners, but it is his words that hold them, for he purposefully brings them face-to-face with the vital issues of their lives: How can they live with one another? How can they find joy? What happens after they die? Why do they suffer?

He also reveals God's truth as it pertains to those issues, and he demands his listeners make decisions and take actions based on that truth. He constantly calls on them to take action — to come, go, follow, heal, repent, pray, *act!*

"You cannot follow me if you want only to be a spectator in life," he warns. "Following me demands full participation in life. Spectators will be left behind."

More than that, the Jews realize his teaching is new. No rabbi has ever said what Yeshua is saying. His teachings do not contradict the Jewish teachings and so his listeners are comfortable with it; yet, somehow, it does not fit within the familiar old teachings. It is born of the old but it is not the old, and the old molds cannot contain it.

Yeshua and the rabbis both assume the existence of one God, and both emphasize God's creative power, his holiness, his majesty, his moral perfection. But the rabbis paint God as a righteous, judgmental, and undefeatable warrior-king who will destroy unfaithful nations. In contrast, Yeshua portrays God as a loving father who wants to do good things for all his children.

Though the rabbis are familiar with that idea — their Scriptures touch on it in several places — no one before Yeshua has ever focused on it. And Yeshua focuses on it closely.

"Our father is so powerful that not only did he create the heavens and earth, and life and light and beauty and music and you and me and everything else that exists, and not only does he keep it all in order, but he is so powerful that he can, and will, and wants to deal with you individually and supply all your needs. God cares when a sparrow falls out of a tree; how much more so does he care about the humans he creates?"

Yeshua teaches as no one before ever has that God is an infinite activity of love. He insists that the whole meaning of humanity, the meaning of creation itself, is rooted in divine love.

He emphasizes, as no one ever has before, the unlimited, merciful and forgiving love of God.

"Yes, God judges people who turn away from him," Yeshua tells the masses, "but he is eager to forgive any transgression committed by anyone who turns to him at any time. Without exception!"

Some listeners also notice Yeshua's teaching differs from — but does not contradict — the rabbis' teaching on perceptions of God.

"God is not a future possibility," Yeshua tells his listeners over and over. "He is not a misty idea. He is a here-and-now reality. I do not speak to you of a God I perceive, but of a God I know."

Such brash statements astound his listeners. Most of them

have heard teachers express their awareness of the reality of God, but never has anyone heard a teacher express that awareness with the level of intensity and certainty that Yeshua does.

"And you, any of you, all of you, can experience the truth of my words for yourselves," Yeshua continues, almost pleading.

"You can do it now. The reign of God is here and now. It is available for everyone. All you have to do to make it your own is to accept it."

As days pass and Yeshua becomes increasingly aware of the Pharisees' impending return, the reign of God becomes his central topic. He speaks of it often. He likens it to a treasure found in a field, and says that whoever finds it should sell everything he has to buy the field. He describes it as a pearl of such great value that its finder should sell everything he has to buy it. He says it would be better to cut off an arm or a foot than to fail to embrace the reign of God.

"It is the one thing needful," he stresses, emphasizing the word "one".

Aware that his time is running out before the Pharisees return, he implores his listeners to understand now the importance of God's reign.

"You can discover the reason for your birth, the purpose of your life, and the hope for your future by understanding and living under the reign of God," he insists.

Often, those who hear him teach approach him with questions. Are you saying. . . ? Will you clarify. . . ? Could you expand. . . ? Does that mean. . . ?

"The reign of God itself is not a new idea to us," one of his Jewish listeners tells him. "We've heard of it all our lives. It was at the heart of Judaism from the beginning, and the prophets' writings gave it its highest expression. But when you talk about the reign of God, you give it a whole new meaning, one that's radically different from what we've always been taught. In fact, everything you teach differs radically from what we've always been taught."

"Actually, that's not quite true," Yeshua replies. "We both teach that God's reign will be established on the initiative of God alone."

"Yes, but that's about all you agree on. The rabbis emphasize that the reign of God will mean national reward and vindication for Israel. They say the scattered tribes will gather, Israel's enemies will be defeated, and everyone will recognize Zion as the center of world rule. But you insist the reign of God is here and now, and anyone can experience it here and now."

"True. The rabbis also imply the reign of God is for Jews alone, but it's for everyone — Jews, gentiles, men, women, kings, slaves, everyone."

"Yes, but another difference is the prophets' insistence that the reign of God will bring a golden age of peace and plenty for everybody," the questioner persists. "Rabbis always emphasize that, but you never do. Why?"

"I don't emphasize it, but I do teach it," Yeshua replies.

"Certainly God provides for his children's material needs, just as he provides for our mental and spiritual needs. I don't emphasize it because relying on material comforts as a foundation for happiness is doomed to fail. Just as too few material comforts can force you to spend all your time toiling for them, and thus make you miss life's higher pursuits, too many material comforts — or even too much effort poured into gaining material comforts — can seduce you away from recognizing

God's face when it appears in front of your eyes. Too much emphasis on the physical leads you away from God and into a hollow life."

"I don't understand your depiction of the Messiah as an agent of God," another questioner interjects. "The prophets said God would someday anoint one person to act as his agent, but they disagreed widely as to what that agent would be like. Today, though, most rabbis agree that the agent will be a great political and military leader. You, however, are the first teacher ever to declare that the Scriptures' passages about the 'suffering servant' apply to the Messiah."

"Yes." Yeshua waits.

"Well, that cannot be. It's ludicrous to even consider the idea that God — especially the God of love you teach about — would anoint someone as his agent, then let that person suffer and die. God would never do that. He would never allow that! It's unthinkable! How can you teach that? It puts into question everything else you teach, for if you can be so wrong on something that important. . . ." His voice trails off as he looks to Yeshua for a reply.

"Even my own disciples try to reject that," Yeshua says quietly. "But it is true and I will keep on teaching it. Someday you will see it. I hope you will understand it then."

Another in the group changes the subject. "The biggest difference I see between you and the rabbis is your insistence on the practical, personal, loving, here-and-now presence of God. All the prophets said that we would recognize the reign of God by an awareness of his presence and obedience to his will. Today, though, although the rabbis don't totally ignore that — and some of them even try to apply it — neither do they make obedience to God's will a prominent feature of the official religion."

"Sadly, the personal, here-and-now relationship with God ceased long ago to be a prominent feature of the temple rulers' teaching," Yeshua replies. "Too much mitigated against it. The threat or the reality of foreign dominance, the corruption in high places, the terrible economic sufferings, the unmerciful toil needed by many just to get through the day — no wonder people showed so little interest in the deeper issues of life! Instead, most people dreamed of an independent homeland, enough to eat, escape from their pain. So, the rabbis began to divert the people's attention away from the grueling realities of their everyday lives by focusing on the Golden Age to come. But my focus is not on the age to come. My focus is on the reign of God, which is here, now, and available to everyone."

Later in the night, after the crowds have dispersed and Yeshua relaxes by the lakeside with his disciples, he reviews the lessons of the day.

"The greatest tragedy in the world is humanity's self-imposed separation from God," he says. "God always does what God says God will do. He always has. He always will. Yet, so many people still won't trust him. All you have to do to prove to yourself that God is trustworthy is to understand what he demands from you and what he promises you, and do as he says. If God does not do what he says he will do, it will prove I am a false teacher. But, if God does what God says God will do, then my teaching must be right."

As the disciples consider what they have just heard, a worried-looking acquaintance of Yeshua slips up beside him and whispers something into his ear. The news draws a curtain of concern over Yeshua's face. He asks a few quick questions, nods that he understands, thanks his caller for coming, and bids him good-bye. Then he calls the four members of his inner circle together.

"Just as we thought," he tells them solemnly, "the Pharisees withdrew only to lay new plans. I've just learned they have allied themselves with the Herodians, and together they are plotting to kill me."

The news shocks the disciples into speechlessness. They expected trouble — Yeshua taught them that lesson very early and very well — but they didn't expect this much trouble. And not this soon. For if the Herodians are involved now, the disciples all realize, they could strike at any moment, day or night, using the multitudes or the darkness as cover. And Yeshua would be dead. A wave of fear sweeps through the disciples as they contemplate their lot.

"Can't you quit teaching?" Andrew asks plaintively. "Can't you do something else and have the same effect?"

"No," Yeshua answers quickly. "My teaching is right. It does not violate any tenet of Judaism. I use new combinations, provide new interpretations, and apply new emphases, but nothing I say challenges anything in the Law. No, the teaching is right, but it attacks the status quo. It shines light on the corruption that organized religion can bring. It is the corrupters who want to silence me. They must not win, so I must continue teaching."

A puzzled look crosses Yeshua's face. He hadn't been expecting this either. After a pause, he continues. "So," he says, speaking more to himself than anyone else, the sound of his voice reflecting the puzzled look on his face, "now I'm the one caught in a dilemma."

When his disciples show signs of not understanding, he explains: "If I continue to teach, the Herodians will kill me, probably very soon. But I will not stop teaching. Soooo... what to do?" His voice trails off as he finishes the sentence.

The disciples are reduced to stammering wonderment as the reality sinks in that Yeshua's choice appears to be stop teaching immediately or die immediately — if, indeed, it is not already too late for him to stop teaching. Maybe he's already as good as dead. Maybe the Herodians are planning their strike tonight. It could come at any moment, from any direction. In the pressure of the moment, the disciples forget their conviction that Yeshua may be the Messiah, and God will protect the Messiah from death.

Yeshua considers his predicament. He cannot imagine quitting his teaching, but neither can he see himself dying in the desert dust with so much work still to do. Yet, he sees no other alternative.

He looks closely at his disciples, and the worry he sees reflected in their faces reminds him that they still do not understand that his teaching is as real as the ground they sit on. They do not understand because they have not experienced, and they have not experienced because they have not fully believed. But they must learn! Before he dies, they must learn!

They are his disciples now, but they must become his apostles. They must understand his teaching so thoroughly that they'll make it their personal own, and live it before all humanity so that everyone will see that the ancient God of the Jews is also the God of all people. By whatever name and by whatever approach, the God of one, the God of love, is God of all. If one life so lived can affect twelve, then twelve can affect a thousand,

and a thousand can affect a million, and humanity will be saved from its own self-destructive ways.

But in order to teach that, Yeshua needs time. Time to teach his disciples. Time to think of a solution to the problem of the Pharisees and Herodians. Time to commune privately with God. Here, however, beside the placid waters of the Sea of Galilee, there is no more time.

"Peter," he suddenly orders. "Get the group ready. We're leaving."

"Where are we going?" a startled Peter asks.

"The shores of the Great Sea, near Sidon and Tyre. We have friends there. It's gentile territory, so neither the Pharisees nor the Herodians will follow us there. We can be alone. I need time and solitude to think."

8

Within the hour, Yeshua and his twelve disciples have slipped out of the Capernaum area without alerting anyone and are walking rapidly toward the Turan Valley.

Yeshua moves quickly and quietly, deep in thought. Is he fooling himself by thinking he could be the Messiah? How could the Messiah be put into a position like this?

He also begins to wonder anew how people perceive him. Those poor, raving people had identified him early on as the Messiah, and they'd shouted that identification everywhere he'd been after that, despite his demands that they stop. Do they believe his words or are they simply mad? Is anyone listening to them? Do many people think he is the Messiah? Or might be the Messiah? What do they say to one another when they talk among themselves?

"Who do people say I am?" he suddenly asks his disciples.

"John the Baptist," Andrew answers.

"Elijah," says Matthew.

"One of the prophets," offers John.

Yeshua ignores the implications of reincarnation in their answers.

"But who do you say I am?" he asks.

"You are the Messiah," Peter answers firmly.

All of the other disciples fall silent as the words hang in the air. Yeshua looks at Peter a long moment, then says quietly but sternly: "Never say that again! Not to anyone!"

Peter nods as the other disciples listen closely.

"A public declaration that I am the Messiah would cause more problems than it could ever solve. It could destroy my ministry, even get me killed."

Andrew's looks startled. "Why? How?"

"For one thing, people would expect me to be their idea of a Messiah, and when I didn't measure up, they would turn away from me. They would never hear me. Also, if people become too concerned about who I am, they will miss why I am here, which is my teaching. And I care far more about my teaching than I do anything else."

"But get you killed?"

"The Sanhedrin could use any proclamation that I am the Messiah as evidence to convict me of blasphemy, which it could twist into a capital crime against Rome — claiming to be a king, for example. Rome could have me crucified for that."

Simon interjects, "Isn't that a little far-fetched?"

"Maybe, but regardless. Do not ever say that I am the Messiah."

Yeshua looks from face to face to emphasize his words, and the disciples understand. Never again will they broach the subject.

שׁ שׁ שׁ שׁ

As the thirteen men make their way westward through the rocky Turan Valley and on to the Great Sea's edge, Yeshua uses the time to teach his disciples the lesson they least want to hear and most want to reject. But they must hear it, understand it, and accept it.

"Even if I escape the Herodians," he begins, "I will have to suffer many things. Very soon the Pharisees, scribes, Sadducees, elders, chief priests — all the temple's leaders — will reject me and seek to have me killed. But, listen to me: Three days later I will rise from the dead and live among you again forever."

The disciples respond as one, with angry disbelief, each one completely rejecting his forecast. "If God is the loving father you're forever telling us he is, then he would never, under any circumstances, let you die such an ignoble death," John cries. "Not you! Not the best teacher he ever had! And as for saying you will rise from the dead and live among us again, well, that's just plain preposterous."

The other disciples vigorously nod their agreement as they openly scoff alongside John. Their minds are closed. They will not listen, so they do not hear.

Over the next few days, Yeshua does everything he can to make his disciples see that truth, but their minds remain shut.

Peter eventually takes Yeshua aside to rebuke him privately.

"Yeshua, you've got to stop saying someone is going to kill you and you're going to rise from the dead. That's nonsense! God would never let anyone kill you — of all people, not you. God will protect you and you know it. So stop this ridiculous talk."

"Get away from me!" Yeshua barks back. "You're setting your

mind on human things, not divine things."

Days pass. Although Yeshua continues to concentrate much of his teaching on his own impending suffering and death, his disciples still refuse to hear it. The very idea of his being killed remains unthinkable to them.

And so, frustrated with his inability to reach his disciples, undecided as to what to do about the Pharisees and Herodians, in wonderment about how to resume his public teaching, and with valuable time passing, Yeshua decides to withdraw farther from civilization for a while.

"I've got to get away and have some time alone," he confides to John. "I've been attending the needs of others so much that I've neglected myself. I need to spend time in solitude so I can find some answers."

"Where will you go?"

Yeshua wants to say Mount Tabor, a 1,800-foot-tall volcanic cone just east of Nazareth. As a younger man he spent many days there, contemplating and meditating, and he feels a nostalgic pull to go there now. But he quickly rejects the idea because Mount Tabor has become too populated, and Yeshua wants solitude. Furthermore, its close proximity to Nazareth would increase his chances of being identified by Nazarenes who still seek to stone him.

"Mount Herman," Yeshua replies after a few seconds. "We'll find a place near the River Jordan's headwaters."

"Will you go alone?"

"I'll need you, James, and Peter with me. Andrew can stay with the others while we're gone."

Yeshua doesn't say it, but he wants his key disciples for companionship and support, and to discuss ideas. He longs for solitude so he can clear his mind of all thought and listen for the voice of God that he heard so clearly at his baptism and in the wilderness. He sees no answer to his dilemma, no breakthroughs. He has done all he can and now he needs guidance.

As Peter prepares for the trip, Yeshua tells his disciples to remain in the Sidon and Tyre area until he returns. Then Yeshua, Peter, John, and James leave for Mount Herman.

The four arrive on the mountain in late afternoon and find a campsite near a spring. Yeshua spends most of the starless night between deep prayer and fitful sleep. The next morning there is no sunrise. Thick clouds blot the sky, and the black night fades into a gray morning.

Yeshua separates himself from the others early so he can be alone. He ambles aimlessly along natural paths that web the mountainside, trying to clear his mind of his problems and focus on God. But his mind only goes in circles: *I cannot stay and I will not leave, but what else can I do? I cannot continue teaching and I will not quit teaching, but what else is there?*

He is physically tired, mentally drained, and spiritually confused. Around noon, he collapses next to a tree on the mountain's south side, and gazes out over an expanse of land toward Jerusalem, one hundred miles away.

Wearily he drops his head into his hands and massages his temples. He sits quietly, absorbing the calming sounds and smells of approaching spring, grateful for nature's miracles that ease the pains that permeate his body and soul.

"What do you want?" he whispers. He hears nothing.

"What do you want me to do?" he repeats.

Still nothing.

He thinks. He prays. Still nothing.

He calls up all the wisdom he can from the Scriptures, focusing especially on the lives and words of Moses and Elijah — Moses because he brought God's Law to the people, and Elijah because God spoke through him with unique directness and clarity. Both had placed their utter trust in God, and both had stepped out boldly into the unknown, depending absolutely on God's promises alone. After that, their lives were filled with peril, but because they persevered, they became two of the greatest leaders Judaism had ever known.

As Yeshua considers their lives, he wonders. *Could it be that God is calling me to such a life? If so, God would lead the way, just as he led Moses and Elijah. I would not — could not — fail.*

The thought eases Yeshua's mind. By mid-afternoon, calm at last, he sits erect on the ground and breathes in deeply, beginning the process that will clear his mind of all thought and help him become preternaturally aware. He prays to hear the voice that spoke to Abram in Ur, Moses on the mountain, and Yeshua at his baptism.

He chants the sounds slowly and repeatedly — "*Ohhhhhreeeeeahhhhhhhmmmmmmnnnnn*" — until he feels his body resonate with his mind. Then, very slowly, he lets Silence take over.

When his eyes open again, it is late afternoon. For a while he sits motionless, his face plainly reflecting the surprise and trepidation that suddenly saturate his mind and soul. He had fully expected answers to his questions, but not these answers.

"Jerusalem?" he hears himself whisper. The astonishment in his voice mirrors the feeling in his heart. Jerusalem is the last place he would have chosen. It is home of his most powerful enemies, the very people who would gain the most from his demise.

As he contemplates the idea of going to Jerusalem, he begins to see genius behind it. And the more he contemplates, the more surprise and trepidation melt from his face and heart, replaced by understanding and joy. The pain of not knowing what to do is over, and relief floods through Yeshua as his new direction settles in.

He hears the music of the spheres that surround him. He looks into the setting sun, which has turned the thick gray clouds into a panoply of yellows, reds, oranges, and purples. He absorbs all the natural piety that engulfs him. He smiles, then grins, widely, as he feels himself cocooned in a love that surpasses his understanding. Soon he can no longer keep the exuberance inside him. He leaps to his feet with a shout of exultation.

"Peter! John! James!" His voice thunders across the mountainside.

The three disciples, who have been waiting nearby, clamber up the mountainside as fast as they can. As they arrive they see Yeshua standing on a ledge, gazing toward Jerusalem. His exultant expression, lighted by the setting sun's red rays, make him appear to glow.

"What? What?" Peter stammers.

"We're taking the ministry to Jerusalem!" Yeshua shouts.

The three look back at him blankly. Peter finally breaks the silence.

"Jerusalem?" he asks incredulously.

"Yes. During Passover."

"Have you lost your senses?" Peter asks, his voice taking on strength as the reality of Yeshua's statement begins to replace the shock.

"No," Yeshua laughs. "It's the best possible place at the best possible time."

"It's the worst possible place at the worst possible time, Yeshua! You'd be walking into the teeth of your most powerful enemies, people who want you dead and have the authority to bring it about. Have you forgotten the Sanhedrin, Yeshua?"

"Jerusalem is the holiest city in the world," Yeshua replies evenly. "And the temple within its walls is the holiest of all manmade structures in the world. That's where I must be."

John starts to interrupt but Yeshua waves him quiet and continues speaking.

"But moreso, I know now that my enemies will try to kill me regardless of what I do. If I remain in Galilee, the Herodians will strike from the dark to murder me and scurry back into the dark after the deed is done. However, if I go to Jerusalem and teach openly in the temple, and the temple powers want to arrest me, they'll have to do it publicly. They'll have to come out into the open, into the light, and explain specifically how my teaching violates either the Scriptures or the Law — which they cannot do because it does neither. Then they'll have to explain just why they want to execute me for teaching the Law and Scriptures accurately."

Yeshua laughs. "The people would riot if they did that."

"That may work for daytime in the temple, but how about nighttime?" Peter fires back, unamused. "You can't teach in the temple all day and all night for seven days, so what would prevent them from coming for you at night when everyone is asleep?"

Yeshua laughs again.

"Because it will be Passover, remember? There'll be more

than two million celebrating people jammed into Jerusalem then. The city never sleeps during Passover. There's never any privacy for anybody. They couldn't arrest me in the street at night any more than they could arrest me in the temple during the day — even if they could find me among two million people."

The three disciples contemplate Yeshua's words and realize he is right. Jews celebrate many feasts, but none like Passover. Passover is a mammoth annual celebration, one full week of worship and joyous feasting, that brings Jews to Jerusalem from all over the world. It recalls the Jews' escape from slavery in Egypt, and it symbolizes, as nothing else does, their reliance on God.

Over the centuries Passover has become so important that every able-bodied male who lives within twenty miles of Jerusalem is required to attend every year, and every Jewish male living anywhere else in the world is required to make the trip at least once in his lifetime.

In actual practice, though, Jews around the world attend Passover as often as they possibly can, and the result is that during this time, the population of Jerusalem swells to many times its usual size, to as many as two and a half million people. During Passover, every street, every corner, every public space, teems with festival goers, day and night. There is no privacy or quiet times, just throngs of constantly moving people.

Yeshua breaks into their thoughts. "Besides," he says, "all those people need to hear my teaching."

The disciples still are not convinced.

"It's too dangerous," Peter argues, again forgetting his conviction that God would protect his Messiah. "One mistake and you're dead. The Sanhedrin already wants you dead, and it can see to it that you die. You know how cozy the Sanhedrin is with Rome. As long as it doesn't cause Rome any problems, it does pretty much as it pleases. Don't sell the Sanhedrin short, Yeshua. If it wants you dead, you're dead."

"There really is no other choice, but don't worry," Yeshua says, his out-of-place smile crinkling his face. "Whatever happens will be fine."

Peter shakes his head in resignation. "Then we're with you all the way."

As the four walk back toward Sidon and Tyre, the disciples notice Yeshua does not appear at all worried, so they also begin to relax. By the time they join the other disciples, they are prepared to help ease the disbelief they expect — and get — at the mention of the word Jerusalem. But in time, just as Peter, John, and James had accepted Yeshua's decision on the mountain, so do the others.

Although they accept Yeshua's plan to go to Jerusalem, they continue to reject the idea that he will have to suffer and die. On that they remain adamantly united. If Yeshua is the Messiah, as they still suspect he is, God would never let him suffer or die.

Yeshua reads their thoughts, but has to let the matter drop for now. He'll have more time during their trip to Jerusalem to try and reach them. For now, though, he has to begin making plans for the trip. He especially has to make plans for Passover, which is less than one month away.

9

Yeshua begins by deciding to follow the shortest, most direct route from Galilee to Jerusalem, even though most Jews avoid that route because it leads through the heart of Samaria. Not only do the roads cut roughly through the hilly country, but Samaria is homeland of the Jews' enemies, the despised, unclean Samaritans.

Most Jews hate Samaritans because seven centuries earlier, during and after the dispersion, they intermarried with gentiles, thus surrendering their racial purity and their standing as Jews and becoming permanently unclean half-breeds. The hatred became so strong over the ensuing years that today no self-respecting Jew will be seen talking with a lowly Samaritan. Most won't even travel in Samaria unless there is no other choice; they prefer detours even if they are longer. Yeshua, however, wants to teach as many people as possible on his trip to Jerusalem, and the most people are in Samaria. Yeshua doesn't care who they are or what their backgrounds are; he cares only that they are people. The reign of God is for everyone.

Once the route is decided, Yeshua sends a team of friends ahead to Jerusalem to set up plans for the Passover week. He needs a place near Jerusalem where he and his disciples can sleep safely at night, a room inside Jerusalem where they can share Passover meals, an ass that has never been ridden, and various other items he intends to use in his upcoming work.

After they are gone, he sends seventy other followers into the towns and villages he intends to pass through on his way to Jerusalem. He instructs them to announce his impending arrival.

He also tells them to take nothing with them, but rather to trust God to provide whatever they need. Because time is short and he needs them to reach as many people as possible, he also tells them to immediately leave any house or any village where they are not welcome. A few days after the group leaves, Yeshua and his disciples follow.

The journey to Jerusalem begins as a leisurely stroll with numerous stops along the way to preach and teach. There is no reason to hurry now. Passover is still two weeks away and, since the trip can be covered in two or three days, Yeshua has time to go slowly.

The seventy followers did a thorough job of letting Samaritans know Yeshua was coming, so throngs of people emerge to greet him along the route. Many have heard him speak in the hills and fields around the Sea of Galilee and want to hear him again. Others have never seen him, but they have heard remarkable stories about him — his personal magnetism, his teaching, his miracles, his ability to heal the sick merely by touching them, his fearless confrontations with the Pharisees — and want to see for themselves if the stories are real.

Yeshua does not disappoint. He fills each day blessing children, teaching, and healing. He shows how anyone can live a God-filled life by telling them parable after parable, spinning simple, clear, colorful stories that show them plainly and simply what God asks of his children and what he promises them in return.

He draws word pictures for his listeners, and tailors each picture to their environments so the morals will be starkly clear and hard to forget. He tells a group of shepherds that God himself is like a good shepherd who will never rest until every one of his sheep is safe. The shepherds, who are devoted to their flock, understand. He tells tenants in the wine country that God is a just landowner who always treats his tenants well. The tenants see the picture. He tells everyone that God is a good father who provides good things for his children, and all his children have to do is accept them.

Yeshua makes entering the reign of God seem simple, but not easy. He tells some farmers that anyone who puts his hand to the plow and looks back is not worthy of the reign of God.

He makes certain that they understand that there is a price for following God. But, he emphasizes that the price is minute compared with the joy it brings. Over and over, in every way he can, he tells people all they have to do to realize that incomparable joy is to trust God and love people.

Yeshua's teaching is not always well received. A rich young man tells Yeshua he is frustrated because his wealth has not brought him the happiness he thought it would.

"I don't know what to do," he says.

"Sell everything you own and concentrate your efforts on loving God and people," Yeshua replies. "If you do so, you will be happier than you can imagine. You'll be joyous!"

The man scoffs. "Do you really think it's that easy?"

"No." The reply is sharp, but not unkind. "It's not easy at all. But it is that simple. Your wealth has become your burden. Lay it down, live as I show you, and let the events that follow speak for themselves."

The young man contemplates Yeshua's words, then slowly shakes his head.

"I'm a wealthy man. Asking me to give up my wealth is asking too much. It's all I have."

As he turns and walks away, carrying his burden, Yeshua watches sadly.

People who depend on wealth to bring them happiness are not alone in rejecting Yeshua's teaching. Many think his ideas are oversimplified, or unprovable, or baseless, or too demanding, or any number of other reasons. Some reject it out of fear, or pride. It saddens Yeshua that they will not attempt to experience his teaching, and thus cannot possibly understand.

Nevertheless, most people are mesmerized by both teacher and teaching. Many of the people, especially women, join his ministry as it moves along its slow route toward Jerusalem. Because women are held in such low esteem in Palestine, they cannot preach for Yeshua as his disciples do, but they serve his ministry in other ways. Yeshua astonishes the orthodox populace by welcoming women into his ministry. Normally, women are accepted mostly for their breeding and domestic qualities, but otherwise are considered useless.

The women who follow Yeshua represent a wide variety of society in Palestine. They range from Joanna, the wife of the top-ranking Roman official who looks after King Herod's financial interests, to Mary Magdalene, a prostitute from the village of Magdala whom Yeshua teaches to feel clean and worthy again, and include every social level in between.

Despite Yeshua's successes, and the huge and enthusiastic crowds he draws, he cannot rid himself of the feeling that he is failing in his mission. Yes, people come. Yes, they listen. Yes, they respond with praises and promises, and excitement and awe and wonderment. But Yeshua knows that as soon as he leaves a village, the excitement he produced will begin to recede, and many of his well-meaning listeners will revert to following the very same gods of mammon that robbed them of their rightful happiness in the first place.

Some of them will test his teaching by living it, however, and he is deeply grateful for them because he knows they will never turn away. They will experience for themselves the inestimable beauty of a life lived for love.

What bothers Yeshua most is his disciples' self-imposed blindness. Sometimes he thinks they are on the verge of understanding, but then something happens that reminds him of how far away from full understanding they really are, as when his cousins James and John approach him to ask him a favor.

"When you come into your glory," James begins hesitatingly, "may John and I have the most important places near you?"

Yeshua stares at his cousins, astonished at their lack of understanding. After all he has been teaching them, they are still looking for an earthly Messiah. If he can't even reach his own hand-picked disciples, whom he teaches every day, how can he ever hope to reach the masses? He pauses before he answers James.

"You don't know what you're asking," he finally says. "I've been telling you these last few days about what's going to happen to me. I'm going to have to suffer horrible pain — physically, mentally, and spiritually. And then I will be murdered. Can you endure that with me? Can you immerse yourself in the hatred, pain, and humiliation I have to face? Can you die a slow and tortured death with me? Because if you really want to share my glory, you will have to share my pain. Can you do it?"

"Yes, of course we can," James says determinedly.

Yeshua nods slowly. "Then you will live my life with me. But, as for your places in my in glory, that's not for me to decide. That's for God to decide."

When John and James have a chance to discuss the conversation later, the other disciples overhear them and become vexed.

"Foul!" cries Judas. "You're taking unfair advantage just because you're his cousins."

Other disciples who overheard the conversation agree with Judas, and begin grumbling among themselves about what their places might be in the coming hierarchy. Yeshua hears the talk and senses a growing jealousy among the disciples, and calls them all together to settle the issue.

"Look," he says, "the standard of greatness in this world is power. The world judges a person by how much money he has, or how many people he controls. But in our world, the standard of greatness is not how much money or service you can extract, or what worldly position you can attain, but rather how much you give and serve. The more you serve the greater you become. So if you wish to be great, be a servant; if you wish to be the greatest, be a slave. That's why I'm here — to be everyone's slave."

"And therefore you'll be the greatest?" Judas blurts, raising his eyebrows sharply.

"The world will judge that," Yeshua says. "But that's not important. What's important is my teaching. It is important that you learn it so you can teach others when I am gone."

Yeshua scans the faces of his disciples and sees that they are thinking, but still not entirely convinced. The Zealots Judas and Simon have especially sour looks on their faces, the same looks they show every time Yeshua tells them Rome is not their biggest problem, or when he tells them that love can defeat anything.

But Yeshua will not give up. He must make them understand so they can live his teaching and demonstrate its power to the world after he is gone. If he can, they will teach others, who will teach others, and the world will change for the better one person at a time forevermore. If he cannot, if his disciples cannot be made to understand, there will be no one to teach the world, his teaching will die, and the world will remain in darkness.

So urgently important does Yeshua consider their understanding that, a few days before Passover, he abruptly cuts short his trip through Samaria, leads his disciples across the River Jordan to its less-populated east bank, and gives them his full attention as they complete their trip to Jerusalem.

He talks to them passionately as they walk, and he intensifies his demonstration of love for them. When they fail to understand the meaning of a parable, he explains it to them. When they fail to understand what his life is about, he elucidates. When they fail him personally, and bicker among themselves, as they often do, he forgives them and continues to shower them with the unconditional love he teaches them to offer others.

Still they will not understand. Instead, they try to make his teaching fit their own preconceived notions. They accept what their intellects and prejudices allow them to accept, but they reject everything that exceeds their sense of logic.

"Listen to me!" Yeshua implores them. "When we get to Jerusalem, the chief priests and legal experts will find a way to condemn me. They'll hand me over to Rome, and Roman soldiers will ridicule me, whip me, torture me. They will kill me! But on the third day I will rise again! You must understand that if you are to become my apostles!"

Despite his efforts, and before Yeshua can break through to them, time runs out. Passover will not wait on the disciples to open their eyes. So, as the Sabbath nears, Yeshua leads his band back across the Jordan River near Jericho, near the spot where John baptized him, and heads toward Jerusalem. They stop at Bethphage, just east of Jerusalem, to spend the last Sabbath before Passover with friends and lay their final plans. Early on Sunday morning, Yeshua is ready to begin what he knows will be the final week of his life — unless God intervenes.

א א א א

He begins Sunday shortly after sunrise by dispatching two of his disciples to obtain an ass that had never been ridden, which his messengers had arranged for. Yeshua wants to ride the ass into Jerusalem because he knows the religious establishment at the temple will interpret it exactly as he wants them to — as his claim to the Messiahship. At the same time, he knows they will do nothing about it.

The prophet Zechariah had written centuries earlier, "Rejoice, O daughter of Zion! Shout aloud, O daughter of Jerusalem! Lo, your king comes to you; triumphant and victorious is he, humble and riding on an ass, on a colt the foal of an ass." By riding into Jerusalem on an ass that had never been ridden, Yeshua would be symbolically declaring his Messiahship.

At the same time, since custom dictates that any king who rides an ass into another king's domain comes in peace versus one who rides a horse comes for war, Yeshua would also be declaring his intentions are peaceful. He knows the Pharisees, Sadducees and other temple officials will not miss his declaration, but they will do nothing about it because their charges would disintegrate as soon as they were stated. How could a person be prosecuted for riding an ass?

Yeshua plans to make his symbolic declaration on Sunday by riding to the temple, then turn around and ride out of Jerusalem. The declaration itself will be enough for the first day. He will return to the temple on Monday to begin demonstrating his claim.

As Yeshua awaits his disciples' return with the ass, he sits on the side of a hill overlooking Jerusalem and gazes lovingly across the dry, hard-packed Kidron Valley to the temple as it gleams gold and creamy white in the early-morning sun. He loves the building. He knows it well from the many feasts he has attended there. It is a mammoth structure, a colossal architectural achievement. The temple proper covers thirty acres atop Mount Moriah, and is surrounded by great porches that rest on thirty-seven-foot-tall pillars cut from solid blocks of marble.

The temple itself is built of white marble that has been covered with gold plates that can be seen for many miles in all directions. Though it is still under construction even as Yeshua gazes at it, it already is one of the grandest buildings the world has ever known.

Yeshua's emotions are deeply mixed as he gazes at it.

"I love the temple," he tells John, "but I despise what its present leaders are doing to it. They're letting its spiritual underpinnings rot, and if they don't make severe changes immediately, the temple is doomed to fall again very soon."

Yeshua feels a certain sadness as he thinks of all the temple means to Judaism, for he fully realizes it is very unlikely that the temple rulers who fouled it so badly will wake up in time to save it.

Still, Yeshua knows what he has to do there and he is prepared to do it. He is bolstered by the idea that he cannot possibly fail; he is doing what God anointed him to do and therefore his success is guaranteed.

At the same time, he also realizes that if he were to look at his situation reasonably and logically, he would have to conclude he cannot possibly succeed. The dangers and pressures he faced in Galilee will be multiplied once he gets to Jerusalem. In Galilee, a few Pharisees and Herodians opposed him and almost killed him, but in Jerusalem they will be joined not only by their brothers, but also by the high priest, the chief priests, the full Sanhedrin and — quite probably — even King Herod Antipas and Rome itself.

So, logically he knows he has no chance, but human logic does not guide him. His task is to do the will of God regardless of what logic tells him, and regardless of the cost. He will do his work. He is quietly praying for the strength to do that work when the disciples arrive with the ass.

"It is time," he says.

The disciples put a cloak on the ass and Yeshua climbs onto its back to begin the trip into Jerusalem.

As he nears the city, throngs of people converge on him. Many of them are from Galilee or other parts of Palestine and know him well. Their excitement rapidly spreads through the Passover crowd, and by the time Yeshua arrives at Jerusalem, the excitement is running high. The crowds cheer him on as if he were their king. Many spread their cloaks on the ground in front of him, as their ancestors had done in ancient times for Jehu when he was proclaimed king. Others cut palm branches and wave them at him, just as their ancestors had done when Simon Maccabaeus entered Jerusalem after a crucial military victory over the Greeks.

"Hosanna!" they cry to Yeshua, using the same expression their ancestors had used to cry out to their king to save them from their distresses.

"Hosanna in the highest!" they cry through him to God, imploring God to save them.

Instead of bolstering Yeshua, the cries sadden him. They imply that, although the people understand his symbolic declaration that he is the Messiah, they badly misunderstand what that means. As evidenced by their cries of "Hosanna," and by laying down their cloaks before him, they still expect the Messiah to come as a king to save them from their terrible hardships and their oppressive servitude to Rome. They still want him to save them; they do not want to save themselves. They want to praise him, but they do not want to follow him. He comes to teach love, live love and therefore demonstrate the unutterable power of love, and he constantly impresses on his listeners that the burden he imposes is light. Still, many of his listeners remain content just to praise him, feel good, and look to him to do their work.

But Yeshua must push on. When he reaches the temple, he says nothing and does nothing. He simply looks at it, turns around, and rides back out of Jerusalem the same way he came in.

But his point is made. The officials see him, and they quickly and accurately read his implied claim to the Messiahship. They do nothing, though, because, as Yeshua well knew, they cannot arrest a man for riding an ass. But they know he'll return soon, and when he does, they'll be ready for him. They've been scheming for him ever since the Pharisees returned from Galilee with their disturbing stories, and they're eager to spring their traps.

10

Yeshua returns to the temple Monday morning on foot. As he crosses the Kidron Valley from the east, the crowds who greeted him on Sunday morning with palm branches and hosannas recognize him. Many fall in excitedly behind him, sensing something important may be about to happen.

He enters Jerusalem at full stride and, as he marches past the Old Pool and the Pool of Siloam, more people join him. By the time he reaches the temple, he has attracted a large and boisterous crowd of supporters.

Yeshua does not hesitate as he approaches the temple. He sees ahead of him in the outer court, the Court of Gentiles, a large commotion. He expected it; he's seen it many times before, and every time it sickens and angers him. The Court of the Gentiles is the only section of the temple where non-Jews are allowed to worship, but temple officials, whose duty it is to protect the house of God for all people, have let the Court of Gentiles become a teeming, corrupt marketplace that renders worship impossible. The temple officials go to great extremes to keep the temple's four inner courts holy, but they use the Court of the Gentiles to cheat Jews and insult non-Jews. Yeshua has complained to the temple authorities many times, but to no avail.

Yeshua strides into the Court of the Gentiles and directly to a table where a moneychanger is at work. He cuts through the crowd that surrounds the table and levels his eyes at the moneychanger.

"You're cheating these people," he booms. "Why?"

The crowd instantly hushes and listens. The moneychanger, caught completely by surprise, is taken aback but quickly recovers.

"We, we have a right to be here," he stammers. "We are licensed by the temple and we serve a legitimate need."

Yeshua smiles a cold smile.

"Yes, of course," he says. The tone of his voice matches his smile. "You're right — as far as you go. The temple only accepts particular types of currency or the highest grade of silver coins, so you are needed to exchange foreigners' money for money the temple will accept."

"Yes, exactly."

"And the temple tax is one-half shekel, or a little more than two days pay for a laborer. Correct?"

"Yes."

"And how much do you charge to make this exchange?"

The moneychanger blanches. He sees where this is going. "About half that," he says nervously.

"So, people pay you one day's wages so they can pay the temple two days' wages. That's exorbitant! That's robbery! And you know it!"

"But the money pays for good things that benefit everybody," the merchant pleads. "They repair roads. They buy the gold plates Herod is covering the temple with. And some of the money goes into the temple's treasury."

"And some goes into your pockets and the pockets of your superiors," Yeshua shouts, keeping his gaze locked onto the moneychanger and letting his anger plainly show.

"We earn a fee for our services, of course."

"You take a ridiculously large fee for your services!" Yeshua retorts, refusing to give the merchant any place to hide.

"And since more than two million people are here for Passover, and since most of them have no choice but to pay your fees, you and your kind make an enormous profit off them. You become wealthy by cheating people, mostly poor people, who come here from all over the world only to worship God. And you're doing it in the name of God! That is blasphemy!"

The merchant stammers, but no words come out. In his heart he knows Yeshua is right. He looks into the crowd for someone to help him, but no one moves.

Yeshua turns his attention away from the moneychanger and levels it on a seller of sacrificial animals at a nearby table.

"And you!" He points straight at the seller as he shouts. "You're worse than he is!"

"You are wrong!" the animal seller shouts back, showing an anger of his own. "We sell animals to people who want to offer God a sacrifice in the temple. But no one has to buy from us! They can bring their animals from home if they want to. Or buy them on the streets."

"And for an animal to be acceptable in the temple, it must be perfect, right?"

"Yes, of course."

"And who judges whether an animal is perfect?"

The merchant pales. "Well, we do. The animal sellers do," he says sheepishly, his confidence suddenly draining.

"And have you ever judged as perfect an animal that was brought in from the outside?"

"Yes, of course." The merchant brightens at his perceived opening, but when he sees Yeshua raise his eyebrows without shifting or softening his gaze he knows he's caught and there is no point arguing.

"Well, sometimes," he mumbles. He furtively searches the faces around him, hoping for help. He sees the temple guards and Sanhedrin members watching from the background, but they don't move. No one moves. He's on his own.

Yeshua speaks: "Sometimes? Rarely! Most of the time you find some reason to reject street animals as imperfect even if they're perfect. When you do, you force the worshiper to get a perfect animal elsewhere. And where can he go to assure he gets a perfect animal?"

"Well . . . we sell them." The merchant is talking to the ground now.

"And how much do you charge for a dove — compared with what the dove sellers in the city charge?"

The animal seller stares at the ground, says nothing.

"About ten or fifteen times their prices?" Yeshua prods.

The seller nods slightly.

"As much as two weeks wages for a laborer — right?"

"Well, yes, but. . . ."

"Two weeks wages for a bird?"

"Yes, but look: These aren't our stalls. They belong to the

family of Annas, the high priest. They're even called the Bazaars of Annas. If you have a complaint, take it to Annas, not us."

Yeshua ignores the reply and jumps up onto a small bench so everyone in the courtyard can see and hear him. "Hear me now," he bellows. "Temple officials at the highest levels are making huge profits by robbing you, especially you who are poor and you who are foreigners. They are doing it in the house of God and they claim to be doing it in the nature of God. But they are not! They are hypocrites! They are blasphemers! They desecrate the temple, the holiest of all holy places in the world, for no other reason than to line their own pockets with money.

"Listen to me, all of you! Did not our greatest prophet, Isaiah, write that, 'My house shall be called a house of prayer for all the people'? These temple rulers have turned it into a home for thieves!"

Without waiting for reaction, Yeshua leaps down from the bench, grabs one end of a moneychanger's table and, with all his might, upends it so violently that coins clatter wildly across the wide stone floors. The moneychangers and animal sellers dive for cover as the Passover crowds who followed Yeshua explode with pent-up glee.

Yeshua ignores the bedlam as he cuts a swath across the court, overturning moneychanging tables and wrecking animal-selling operations as he goes. The merchants cower as he scatters their wares and leaves pandemonium in his wake.

Hundreds of confused, frightened doves flutter free from their cages and circle high overhead. A few merchants group together to try to stop him, but he picks up a whip he sees on a table and snaps it hard over his head as he walks toward them. The merchants shrink back.

"Shall we arrest him?" a nervous guard captain yells over the din to a ranking Sanhedrin Sadducee who is watching from a safe distance.

"No!" The Sadducee barks. "If you arrest him now the people will riot. Leave him alone."

The guard retreats to his troops, but a Pharisee who overheard the exchange turns to the Sadducee.

"But we have to arrest him," the Pharisee pleads, alarm in his voice. "We can't just let him wreck the temple."

"No!" the Sadducee barks again. "Yeshua wants us to arrest him. If we accuse him of desecrating the temple we'll have to try him for that, and if we try him for that he'll end up making the rabble believe we're stealing their money. You heard him. You see the rabble. In their eyes he'd be right and we'd be defenseless. Besides, as I told the guard captain, if we arrest him now the people will riot. Look at them."

They turn their attention back to the yelling, clapping, crowd. Yeshua's followers, many of whom are certain they are witnessing the Messiah's opening volley, are letting their jubilance erupt, and they cheer Yeshua on wildly.

The Sadducee turns back to the Pharisee and shouts again, "Don't worry; we'll get him. We're laying for him."

Both return their attention to the pandemonium before them, but they do nothing.

Yeshua throws down the whip and picks up one of the tables he has wrecked. Holding it high over his head, he charges toward a gate on the temple's eastern side. He throws the table down in front of the open gate, then starts piling other tables and benches — whatever debris he can find — with it.

This time it's the gentiles' turn to erupt with emotion. Most of the Jews in the crowd are lost in puzzlement over Yeshua's action, but gentiles immediately understand it and explode with ecstacy. A Jew, a very powerful Jew, is standing up for them against the temple rulers. Rarely does a Jew defend them publicly, and never has a Jew, especially so powerful a Jew, taken their side so strongly. Years of pent-up emotion explode from them as Yeshua quickly and effectively barricades the gate.

When it is big enough, Yeshua grabs a bench and races to a passageway that leads from the Court of the Gentiles to the Court of Women. He crashes the bench down beside a large sign that reads, "Death To Any Gentile Who Passes This Point" — the same sign is at every passageway that leads from the Court of Gentiles into the covered parts of the temple — and stands on the box to speak again. He's calmer now, but still speaks in a loud, commanding voice as he explains his actions to non-comprehending Jews.

"The Court of the Gentiles is the only place in the temple where non-Jews are allowed to worship. That's why temple rules forbid the court's use as a shortcut between the Lower City and the Mount of Olives. It creates a heavy flow of traffic, which renders worship here almost impossible. Yet, despite the rules, temple leaders allow the shortcut to remain open, thus they deny gentiles their rightful place of worship at the temple. This is just one more way the temple rulers desecrate your temple."

With that, Yeshua jumps down from the bench and blows out of the court, away from the temple. He has made his point. He has publicly challenged the temple officials' authority and threatened their purses — and, he knows, sealed his own fate. If his enemies don't stop him now, permanently stop him, he will wreck them and their privileged lifestyles as surely as he wrecked the merchants' tables. He knows it and they know it.

And if the only way to stop him is to kill him, Yeshua knows they will.

Nevertheless, as soon as the temple settles down after his one-man rampage, he returns to spend the afternoon teaching and healing in the temple precincts. He is only slightly surprised when the temple officials offer no resistance. He doesn't even see them, and he assumes they are clustered somewhere to scheme their final plans to trap him.

In late afternoon, Yeshua and his disciples leave the temple, lose themselves in the teeming crowds, then vanish to their campsite near Bethany. Yeshua specifically chose this area because it would be virtually impossible for the temple guards to find him here at night amid all the confusion of the Passover throngs. If they want to arrest him, he will make it easy for them to do it publicly in the daylight, but not secretly under cover of darkness.

When Yeshua returns to the temple Tuesday morning to continue teaching, a delegation from the Sanhedrin — chief priests, elders, and experts in the Law — are eagerly waiting to spring their trap. They don't even wait for him to begin teaching before they attack.

"Tell me," a chief priest says easily, "by what authority do you cause such havoc in the temple as you did yesterday? Who gave you the authority?" He folds his arms confidently and waits on an answer.

Yeshua instantly recognizes the trap. If he says he is acting on God's authority, the officials will claim God would never approve of anyone wrecking God's house and will charge him with blasphemy. If he says he is acting on his own authority, they will claim he is a megalomaniac and arrest him before he causes any more damage. Either way he answers, he is doomed.

Yeshua looks sadly at his questioner for a long moment before he replies.

"I will ask you one question," he says quietly. "Answer me, and I will tell you by what authority I do these things."

The chief priest shuffles slightly, but says nothing.

Yeshua continues: "Did the baptism of John the Baptist come from heaven or was it of human origin?"

The chief priest looks puzzled as the others freeze.

"Wait one moment," he tells Yeshua as he motions for his colleagues to gather around him.

"He's got us," he whispers to them. "We can't say John's baptism came from heaven because the Sanhedrin ignored John's baptism. Even worse, if we say John's baptism came from heaven, Yeshua could say that since John pointed people to him, he is divinely attested."

"Yes," agrees a priest, "but neither can we say John's baptism was of human origin because that would alienate the masses who consider John a prophet."

"Any ideas?" the chief priest asks.

The group members look furtively from one to another, but no one offers an option. No one has an answer. When no one speaks after several seconds, the chief priest breaks the huddle and looks seethingly at Yeshua.

"We don't know," he says.

"Then neither will I tell you by what authority I do these things," Yeshua replies.

The officials feel the sting especially sharply. With one simple question, Yeshua has turned their trap against them, weakened their prestige in the eyes of the masses, and left the implication that both his and John's authority come from God.

The officials are wounded, but they don't give up.

"Then what sign can you show us for doing this?" the chief priest presses.

"Destroy this temple and in three days I will raise it up," Yeshua replies without hesitating.

The priest guffaws. "This temple has been under construction for forty-six years. You claim you could raise it up in three days?"

Yeshua says nothing, and the priest lets the matter drop.

There is nothing the temple officials can do about Yeshua for the time being, so while he begins teaching, the priest decides to retreat before he and his colleagues lose any more face.

As soon as they leave, though, they begin scheming another trap — and this time they determine not to be so clumsy. Yeshua is cleverer than they had expected, so this time they enlist the help of some Herodians. By the afternoon, they are ready. They find Yeshua still teaching in the temple.

"Teacher," a smiling Herodian politely says to him. "We know you are sincere and show deference to no one, for you regard people with impartiality and teach the way of God in accordance with truth. Tell us, is it lawful to pay taxes to the emperor or not? Should we pay them, or should we not?"

Yeshua sighs. Another clumsy trap. If he says the tax is lawful, he will alienate the Jewish masses who hate the tax because it symbolizes Rome's tyranny over them. On the other hand, if he says the tax is not lawful, Roman soldiers will arrest him on charges of sedition and harboring revolutionary intentions against Rome. Yeshua glares at the Herodian, the grinning temple officials who back him, and the temple guards who stand ready to arrest him. Their bumbling traps are becoming tiring, and their hypocrisy infuriates him. This time he lets his anger show.

"Why are you putting me to the test?" he snaps. Before they can answer, he commands: "Bring me a denarius and let me see it."

The Herodian produces the Roman coin and hands it to him. Yeshua glances at it, then holds it up high over his head so everyone can see it.

"Whose face is depicted here?" he asks.

"The emperor Caesar's," they answer in unison.

"Then give to Caesar the things that are Caesar's, and give to God the things that are God's." He smiles at the Herodian, hands him back the coin, and turns back to his teaching.

The crowd of temple officials who had come to watch Yeshua's demise, mostly Pharisees and a few Herodians, retreat once again.

"But we cannot give up," a priest later tells a gathering of Sadducees. "If we can't trap him, we can't . . . get rid of him. And if we don't get rid of him, he'll wreck us all."

"Allowing Yeshua to continue cannot be an option," a Pharisee adds darkly.

"Agreed," replies a Sadducee. "And since we Sadducees have the most to lose if he continues, we'll take over the questioning."

"How?"

"We've already decided what to do if you failed. We'll present him with a hypothetical situation, then ask him a theological question based on that situation." The Sadducee grins smugly before he continues. "But, the question is worded in such a way that regardless of what Yeshua answers, he will look inept and foolish in the eyes of his adoring masses."

"But don't you need our help?" the Pharisee asks.

"No, this we'll do alone."

He does not explain why the Sadducees will do it alone but the Pharisee understands: The question involves theology, and though the Sadducees and Pharisees work closely together, they differ radically in some aspects of their theologies. The Sadducees base their beliefs directly on Mosaic Law, where the Pharisees base theirs largely on the scribes' interpretations of the Law. Sometimes, the result is a clash of theologies.

Such is the case now. The Sadducees plan a question based on immortality, a concept the Pharisees accept but the Sadducees reject because they find no evidence for it in pure Mosaic Law. Because their question to Yeshua will involve a clear understanding of the pure Law, they decide to attempt this alone.

The Sadducees, followed at some distance by some Pharisees and other temple officials eager to witness Yeshua's downfall, find him on Wednesday morning, sitting inside the temple and teaching earnestly. A priest interrupts, ignoring the session that is under way.

"I have a question, Teacher," he loudly declares. Yeshua stops teaching in mid-sentence, looks at him, and waits.

"You are aware of the institution called levirate marriage, are you not?"

"Yes."

"The regulations for levirate marriages stipulate that if a man dies without a child, his oldest brother will take the widow as his wife. If the brother dies childless, the next oldest brother will become her husband. Theoretically, the system repeats itself until the woman bears a child or there are no more brothers."

"Yes. The point is to insure that a family's name continues and property remains within the family."

"Well, yes, that's true. But let's suppose that, in accordance with the regulations governing levirate marriage, a woman marries seven brothers in succession, each of whom dies without fathering a child. Then she dies. If the dead are resurrected, as you teach they are, whose wife will she be in the resurrection?"

The Sadducees all sit back as they anticipate Yeshua's reply, for regardless of what he says, he'll look foolish. His belief in eternal life will look ridiculous, and the rabble will see him for the fraud he really is.

Yeshua is weary of their stupid little games. "You don't know what you're talking about," he snaps. "And the reason you don't know is that you don't know the Scriptures and you don't know the power of God."

The Sadducees recoil, but before they can say anything, he continues. "As for your question about marriage in heaven, when we rise from the dead we become like the angels so we do not marry as we do here.

"And as for eternal life, read your own Scriptures. Remember what Moses wrote in his story of the burning bush? He wrote that God said to him, 'I am the God of Abraham, the God of Isaac, and the God of Jacob.' He said 'I am,' not 'I was.' He spoke of the present, not of the past. So God is not a God of the dead. He is God of the living."

Yeshua abruptly turns away from the Sadducees in disgust and breathes a quick prayer of gratitude that God calls on him to love everyone, not like everyone. He dislikes these Sadducees intensely. They are hate-filled, greedy, complacent hypocrites, and their foolish traps further reveal them as being ignorant as well.

Yeshua turns back to the group he was teaching before the Sadducee interrupted.

"Of all the ways that exist to interfere with the work of God in this world, hypocrisy is the worst," he tells them. "Hypocrisy mocks God. Hypocrisy leads to cynicism, and cynicism drains joy from life. It renders life a dim shadow of what it can be, of what God wants it to be. And hypocrisy among the temple's leaders is worst of all because it robs the temple of its vitality and, therefore, it robs you of your temple. Hypocritical religious leaders steer you away from God by passing off lies as truth."

Yeshua abruptly stands up and climbs atop a table so he towers above the crowd and can be seen and heard by everyone. He motions to a knot of Pharisees who have come to watch the Sadducees trap him, and he roars his words so everyone can hear him clearly.

"Listen to what the scribes and Pharisees tell you about the great principles of the Law and act on those principles, for they are knowledgeable people and they speak rightly of reverence for God and respect for humanity.

"But do not act as they act, for they do not behave as they speak. They heap heavy burdens on you with their endless rules and regulations, but they do nothing to relieve you of your burdens."

Yeshua points straight at his accusers as he continues, his anger rising with every word.

"Look at them and see them for what they are! They are

hypocrites! They use Godly words, but they don't live Godly lives. They give themselves pompous titles, wear pious garments, decorate themselves with gaudy religious trinkets, accept places of honor everywhere they go — in the temple, in the synagogues, at meals, everywhere — but they do it to draw attention to themselves, not to advance the causes of God. They care more about themselves and their appearances than they do about you and your souls."

Now Yeshua spins and faces his accusers directly. "Hypocrites!" he shouts at them, his voice at once a mixture of savage denunciation and poignant sorrow. "You pretend to lead people to a society where God's will is perfectly done, but in truth you block the path that leads there. You claim you roam the earth to convert lost people into followers of God, but in truth you pervert them for your own narrow and rancid purposes. And by your actions you lead them away from God."

The scribes and Pharisees cower under Yeshua's sudden onslaught, but he does not let up.

"You are the worst sort of hypocrites," he thunders. "Your words proclaim your allegiance to God, but your actions testify of your devotion to mammon. You go to extreme lengths to display your faithfulness to the Law in all its fine detail, but in all important matters you show no thought of justice and no sense of mercy.

"Pharisees and scribes, you are hypocrites! You keep all the temple's furnishings clean and shining, but you don't care how those furnishings were obtained — whether by lying, cheating or stealing. You are like a cup that is clean on the outside but filthy on the inside, and what use is that? You are like the tombs of the prophets that you keep so meticulously clean on the outside, but inside they are rancid and decayed, deadly to anyone who touches them.

"You are murderers! You erect tombs for the prophets and you take great care of them, and you claim that had you been alive with the prophets you would have protected them and all other godly people from being slain. But the truth is, you would not have protected them; you would have murdered them, just like you still murder those who follow the prophets' footsteps. You try to murder their spirits, and if that fails, you murder their bodies."

As he ends his rebuke he glowers at his accusers and waits for a reply, but none comes. He is met with utter silence. No one dares say a word. As he scans the crowd, however, a scribe catches his eye. Yeshua recognizes him as a lawyer who had been among the Pharisees when they tried to trap him in Galilee, but it's plain from the expression on the scribe's face now that he is no longer trying to do that. Yeshua senses no antagonism from him, but perceives he is bothered by a sincere question. Yeshua looks at him inquisitively and speaks to him in a non-committal tone.

"Yes?" he says.

The scribe is surprised that Yeshua noticed him in the crowd, because he does have a question.

"Which commandment is the first of all?" he asks.

The question surprises Yeshua. It's a good question. It is straightforward, honest, not antagonistic, and it cuts straight to the core of everything that Yeshua is. Yeshua needs no time to formulate his answer.

"The first is, 'Hear O Israel: The Lord our God, the Lord is one. And you shall love the Lord your God with all your heart, and with all your soul, and with all your mind, and with all your strength.'"

The scribe smiles as he recognizes the ancient, familiar words of the *Shema* and the *V'Ahavta,* the words that have defined the heart and soul of Judaism since the beginning.

But Yeshua does not stop there. He continues, "The second is this: 'You shall love your neighbor as yourself.' There is no other commandment greater than these. Obey them, and everything else will fall into place for you."

The scribe rubs his chin thoughtfully. "I recognize the words," he says. "They come from the writings of Leviticus. But no one has ever put them together with the *Shema* to form a single thought. I'm a lawyer; I'm a scribe. I know what I'm talking about. But you've done more than that. You've shifted the emphasis of the passage ever so slightly, but in doing so you've infused the words with a meaning that is utterly new. When our rabbis refer to a person's neighbor, they mean his Jewish neighbor. But you expand that. You seem to include all people. You seem to leave out no one, not even gentiles or women."

"That is correct," Yeshua says.

The scribe rubs his chin again as he thinks deeply. Yeshua remains noncommittal, saying nothing but watching intently.

"You're right, Teacher," the scribe finally says. His voice and manner are humble. "Loving God and loving our neighbors, whoever they may be, is much more important than all the burnt offerings and sacrifices."

Yeshua smiles. The scribe understands. "You are not far from entering the reign of God," he says.

Before the Sadducees can leave, Yeshua shifts his attention

back to them. "Let me ask you a question," he says, his voice now more curious than angry. "What is your opinion about the Messiah? Whose son is he?"

"David's son," they all reply firmly, grateful for an easy, non-threatening question. The Scriptures are very clear abou whose son the Messiah will be.

Yeshua continues: "Then how can David call the Messiah 'Lord,' as when David said, 'The Lord said to my Lord, sit on my right hand until I put your enemies beneath your feet.' If David calls the Messiah 'Lord,' then how can the Messiah be David's son?"

Once again the Sadducees are left in silence. They have no answer. Yeshua lets the silence hang in the air for a few seconds, then smiles at the Sadducees and returns to his teaching as the temple officials melt into the crowd and disappear.

"We're not going to trap him; he's too quick and too knowledgeable for that," the chief priest grumbles to a cohort after they are a safe distance away.

"But there must be a way," his friend replies.

"Yes, but this time it must be foolproof. We must find a way to bring him before the Sanhedrin without any further public confrontations."

"How is that possible? He surrounds himself with the rabble during the day and he hides at night. What can we do?"

"I don't know, but we'll find a way. We have to."

While the Sadducees and Pharisees plot Yeshua's death, Yeshua spends the afternoon teaching love. Later, as Yeshua leaves the temple, some of his disciples look back in awe at it.

"What an incredible building," Peter remarks. "No other building in the world can compare with it."

Yeshua looks back with them, and a sadness sweeps over him. "True," he says. "But its strength is in its spirit, not in its stones and mortar. If its spiritual underpinnings crumble, the temple itself will soon follow. And I see no sign that the temple leaders have any thought of doing what they must do to prevent it."

"Which would be?"

"Which would be to turn themselves around and put God ahead of their own greed."

"But Yeshua, the temple is too big and too strong to fall. It's indestructible! Surely you're not saying. . . ."

Yeshua cuts him off. "I tell you truthfully, not one stone will be left here upon another. All of them will be thrown down."

After Yeshua is certain he is not being followed, he leads his disciples to the home of an old friend in Bethany to share an evening meal. While they recline around the low table, all of them lying on their left sides and leaning on their elbows as they eat, as is their custom, a woman approaches Yeshua. She stands over him, opens an alabaster vial of ointment, and pours the entire bottle over his head. Then she breaks the bottle to indicate she has no more to give.

Yeshua smiles appreciatively at the woman.

"Thank you," he says kindly.

But he's the only one in the room who shows appreciation. All his disciples, especially Judas, are plainly troubled by the gesture. Judas is outraged.

"Why did you do that?" he exclaims furiously at the woman, ignoring Yeshua's implied approval of her gesture. "That's nard you just poured on him. A single vial of nard can cost a working man a full year's pay! It's extremely rare, and yet you poured a whole bottle on him. It could have been sold and the money given to the poor!"

Some other disciples start to join Judas' attack as the woman withers, but Yeshua stops them.

"Leave her alone! Why do you trouble her? It is a lovely thing she has done to me. You will always have the poor with you and you can help them any time you please, but you will not always have me."

"A few drops of perfume on a visitor's head is customary," Judas fires back, unmoved by Yeshua's explanation. "No one would object to that. But an entire bottle? Of nard? This oil is made from a rare plant found only in India, and pouring a whole vial of it on you is incredibly wasteful! It is indefensible!"

"Is it not customary to anoint a dead man's body with perfume before it is buried?" Yeshua asks.

"Yes, but. . . ."

"And is it not also customary to break the vial the perfume came in and lay the fragments in the tomb with the body?

"Yes, but. . . ."

"This is what she has done for me in advance of my death. She has done for me what she can. She has anointed my body beforehand against my burial."

Judas still is not moved. "It was an extravagant waste and you know it! Both of you should be ashamed of yourselves!"

Yeshua is just as adamant. "I tell you truly," he says evenly, "wherever the good news shall be proclaimed throughout the world from this day forward, the story of what this woman did today will be told so that she will always be remembered."

The words infuriate Judas. He leaps to his feet without another word and storms blindly out of the building. Peter rises to bring him back, but Yeshua stops him.

"Let him go," Yeshua says. "He must to do what he must do."

Simon, however, Judas' compatriot in the Zealots, slips out of the room and tries to calm Judas down.

"There's no need to get so upset over a vial of nard," he says.

But Judas will not be placated. "It's not just the nard," he boils. "It's Yeshua! First he promises he's going to save the world. He keeps telling us that's his calling — and ours! Look around you, Simon. Do you see the world being saved? Do you see hunger vanishing? Do you see Rome retreating? All I see is Yeshua stirring up unnecessary trouble with people who have the power to kill us all."

"But. . . ."

"And even more important than that is his failure to demonstrate that he's the Messiah."

"He's never claimed to be the Messiah," Simon quickly reminds him.

"No, but he's never denied it, either. And he makes a point of doing things everywhere he goes to make people think he's the Messiah, as when he rode that ass to the temple, or when he calls himself 'son of man.'"

"Well, that's true, but. . . ."

"What has he done to demonstrate that claim, Simon? Name one thing he's done to prove his implications."

"Well. . . ."

"Furthermore, he keeps making us think something important is going to happen in Jerusalem during Passover. He's been doing that ever since he came back from Mount Herman. But Passover is one day away, and aside from a few meaningless little verbal clashes with the temple rulers, what has happened? Nothing! Absolutely nothing! Nothing has happened, nothing is happening, and nothing is going to happen."

Simon remains silent as Judas, seething, presses his head against a tree.

"*Damn* him for not acting!" Judas suddenly explodes. "*Damn* him for not listening to us! If he had listened to you and me in the beginning, Simon, things would be different now. God would be with us, the masses would be behind us, and we would have stormed Jerusalem by now. We would have destroyed Rome's stranglehold on Palestine, ended corruption in the temple, and established God's reign on Earth once and forever. Jews would be free of foreign domination. We'd really have something to celebrate on Passover. But instead of listening to us, Yeshua surrounds himself with people who tell him what he wants to hear. He's got all the others — especially Peter, John and James — believing that love is all that's needed. Hah!"

"Why don't you talk with Yeshua about this?" Simon asks.

Judas' laughter sounds like a snarl. "Love obviously is not all that's needed, Simon. Not in the real world. In the real world, men have to take matters into their own hands or nothing will ever change."

"What are you saying, Judas?"

"I'm saying that if Yeshua won't act on his own and no one else will make him act, I will. I'll compel him to act. I'll leave him with no choice but to drop his pretenses and be what his actions proclaim and his words don't refute. I'll make him *BE!* the Messiah! I'll force him!"

"Are you sure you know what you're doing, Judas?" Simon asks nervously.

"Yes! Go back inside and join the others. I'll see you later."

Judas vanishes into the night and heads straight for Jerusalem. He walks rapidly and tirelessly. There is purpose in his step. Matters are in his hands now.

He enters the same gate Yeshua entered when he rode the ass to the temple and, without hesitating, heads straight for the home of the high priest, Caiaphas. As he approaches, a temple guard blocks his path, but before the guard can say anything Judas speaks.

"Take me to Caiaphas," he tells the guard. "I have information."

Thirty minutes later, Judas and Caiaphas have a deal: Judas will lead Caiaphas' men to Yeshua after dark Thursday night when Yeshua is away from the protecting crowds. The deal gives Caiaphas the opportunity he needs to arrest Yeshua at a time and place the rabble cannot see him, thus averting a riot. It gives Judas the opportunity he needs to force Yeshua's hand. Judas even offers to supply the Sanhedrin with all the witnesses it wants to testify against Yeshua in a blasphemy trial. After that, Yeshua will have no choice other than act. He will have to show himself as the Messiah and start saving the world. Yeshua can thank Judas later. For now, Caiaphas seals the deal by giving Judas a token payment of silver. Judas promises he will return Thursday night, then leaves the temple.

11

On Thursday morning, Yeshua stays away from the temple. It is the day of preparation for the Passover feast and there is much he needs to do before the night falls. He plans to share the meal with his disciples and he wants it to be special, so he dispatches several disciples to obtain everything the ancient ritual calls for: a lamb, to remind participants how lamb's blood was used when the angel of death passed through Egypt; unleavened bread, to remind them of the bread their forefathers ate in haste as they escaped from Egypt; saltwater, to remind them of the tears they shed and the Red Sea that parted for them to escape; bitter herbs, to remind them of the bitterness of slavery; a paste-like mixture of fruits and nuts, to remind them of the bricks they made while in slavery; and four cups of wine, to remind them of the four promises God made to the Jews, as recorded in the Book of Exodus — that God would bring them out from under the burdens of the Egyptians, rid them of their bondage, redeem them, and be their God.

It is especially important to Yeshua that he be mentally prepared for the feast, for he knows Judas has betrayed him. It is evident to Yeshua from the way Judas suddenly avoids making eye contact with him, displays unusual shortness with the other disciples, keeps to himself, and appears preoccupied. He has lost sight of the joy of Passover.

Yeshua has known for a long time that Judas rejected his teaching. He's seen it in many little things, but most obviously in the way Judas frowns and clamps his arms across his chest whenever Yeshua disdains talk of becoming a military leader, or when he insists Rome is not the source of the Jews' problems, or when he teaches that loving God and other people is the most important action any person can take.

More than anything else, though, it was Judas' extreme, unbalanced reaction to last night's incident with the nard that signaled to Yeshua that his rejection had turned to betrayal.

And, since it is now Thursday morning, Yeshua knows the betrayal will have to manifest itself very soon, probably tonight, for there will be no other chance. Yeshua will be protected by the daylight today and Friday, and after six o'clock Friday evening it will be too late. The Sabbath begins then, and there can be no arrests on a Sabbath. Yeshua would be safe until the Sabbath ends at six o'clock Saturday, at which time he could lose himself among the more than two million Passover celebrants until it was time to leave Jerusalem.

That leaves tonight, Yeshua surmises, concluding his arrest must be imminent. Pictures of the cross' horrors sweep through Yeshua's mind and he has to force himself to think instead about the Passover supper. He still has not reached his disciples fully, and the supper will be his last chance.

He is ready by six o'clock. For the occasion, his friends secured the upper room of a house in the heart of Jerusalem, in the shadow of Caiaphas' house and less than a five-minute walk from the temple. It has a private entrance from the street so Yeshua and his disciples can come and go as they wish without going through the main house.

As they begin eating, however, Yeshua astounds his disciples by suddenly announcing: "One of you who is sitting here and eating with me will betray me."

The disciples look at one another in dismay, then John speaks.

"Yeshua, we are all your friends. We've traveled some dangerous roads with you, and we've stood with you at every turn. Sure we have disagreements with you, but none of us would ever even think of betraying you."

"One of you twelve will betray me," Yeshua replies. "And nothing but sorrow will come to him for doing so. It would be better for that man had he never been born."

The disciples look worriedly at one another. No one suspects anyone. Judas hides in that darkness.

"Who is he?" Peter demands indignantly. "We have a right to know."

However, when Yeshua sees that Judas intends to stay hidden, he abruptly changes the subject and focuses everyone's attention on the detailed ritual that is the Passover meal.

He closely follows the meticulously detailed, seventeen-step ritual, but toward its end, where the ritual calls for communicants to eat the last of the unleavened bread and drink the fourth and final cup of wine, he departs from the prescribed ceremony to infuse it with a whole new meaning he knows the disciples will never easily forget.

"As you eat this bread," he says solemnly, breaking it and passing it to them, "be aware that just as this bread is broken for you, so is my body to be broken for you."

The disciples eat the bread in silence. Yeshua pours the fourth cup of wine, the cup that recalls the ancient covenant between God and his people. He passes the cup to them and continues.

"Just as this wine is poured out for you, my blood will be shed for you. Let the wine symbolize the blood I shed for you. Let it be the very life of the new covenant."

"The new covenant?" John whispers, his eyebrows rising.

"The old covenant — 'I will be your God and you will be my people' — depends wholly on obedience to the Law," Yeshua says quietly. "The new covenant that I bring you depends wholly on love, or on 'the blood I shed for you.' It means that you don't have to live under the Law of God anymore, for as children of God you can live within his love. There are no rules to follow, no laws to obey. There is only love to be lived."

The disciples sip their wine in deep contemplation. After a few moments, Yeshua returns to the prescribed ritual by leading the twelve in singing The Great Hallel (Psalm 136) and reciting the two short, formal prayers that end the ritual.

It is dark as they step outside the building. Yeshua and eleven of the disciples quickly make their way out of the city without being seen. Only Judas remains behind.

Instead of going to their camp near Bethany, Yeshua leads his disciples out of Jerusalem through a southeastern gate, then turns north and follows a road that parallels Jerusalem's walls.

As they walk, he hears his disciples muttering among themselves about his statement that one of them would betray him, but Yeshua says nothing. When the group nears the temple's outer wall, Yeshua turns abruptly off the road and leads his disciples up a Mount of Olives slope.

"The mount is special," Yeshua whispers to John as they leave the road.

John knows it is. It is one of the very few places around Jerusalem where gardens grow. Jerusalem proper has no gardens because a law forbids spreading manure on holy ground, so wealthy residents often buy parcels of land on the Mount of Olives where gardens are welcome. The result is that an abundance of gardens cover the mountainside.

"A friend of mine owns a garden on the mount's lower slope, an olive grove called the Garden of Gethsemane," Yeshua continues. "He told me I could use it any time I needed it — and I need it now more than ever."

After the group is several yards off the road, Yeshua stops in a clearing and turns toward Peter.

"There's something you want to say, Peter?" he asks.

"Yes," Peter replies. "You said one of us would betray you. None of us would betray you, Yeshua. Like John said, we are your friends as well as your disciples. I am amazed and hurt that after all we've been through together, you would question any of our loyalties."

A murmur of agreement riffles through the group. Yeshua scans their faces in the moonlight, and there is silence.

"You will all fall away from me," he says.

"No!" Peter protests. "The others may fall away, but not me."

Yeshua smiles sadly at him, then speaks to the group. "You are all good men, and you all mean well. I know that. I chose you. You are my friends and I love all of you deeply, but I also know I may have to die on the cross so my teaching will live. And you, as well-intentioned as you are, are not strong enough to follow me to the cross. At some point you will all fall away from me."

Protestations of "No!" and "Never!" and "Not me!" roll through the group.

"When will you die?" Andrew asks.

"Unless God intervenes and saves my life, I have less than a day."

The prediction stuns the disciples. Yeshua has told them many times he must die, but this is the first time he has mentioned a specific time. The sheer brevity of time left makes the prediction seem all too real.

"The only way they can silence me is to kill me, but if I'm not dead by the Sabbath, fewer than twenty-four hours from now, I'll be gone from Jerusalem and they won't have another chance at me. They know that and they cannot allow it to happen. It could ruin them. So, I must go to the cross soon, and you will not follow me there."

Yeshua turns his attention to Peter and looks at him fondly, if sadly.

"Peter," he says quietly, "this night, before the cock crows twice, you will deny me three times."

"Never!" Peter exclaims, horrified at the very thought that he would deny his dearest friend and leader. "I will die with you, but I will never deny you."

All the disciples vigorously echo Peter's thoughts, but Yeshua continues to smile a sad, private smile. When they become quiet again, Yeshua changes the subject.

"Peter, James, John, come with me. The rest of you stay here while I pray."

Yeshua and his inner circle move a little farther into the olive grove, then Yeshua stops again.

"My soul is grieving," he tells the three. "I have to be alone now to pray. Stay here and watch."

As his three closest friends settle down, Yeshua walks deeper into the garden, and as soon as he is out of their sight he falls to his knees beside an ancient, gnarled olive tree. He looks toward Jerusalem and, though the olive trees block it from his sight, he can see the glow from the campfires of more than two million Passover celebrants.

He closes his eyes and begins to pray. He prays so hard, so intently, that great drops of sweat break out on his forehead. But this time he does not pray for understanding, or strength, or direction, or insight, or his friends, or his enemies. This time he prays only for himself. He pleads for an escape from the cross, for he knows if God does not intervene and save him, he soon will be stripped naked, flogged viciously, nailed to a wooden post and hanged out in the sun for however long it takes to die.

Yeshua presses his forehead to the cool earth as he pleads with God for escape. "Father," he cries out, "please, I don't want to die — not like this. Please let there be another way! Surely there's another way!"

He lifts his eyes and searches the night sky for some sign of reassurance, but he sees nothing that offers hope. If God is listening, he is not showing it.

Yeshua presses his head to the ground again and writhes in mental and spiritual agony. Everything seems hopelessly bleak now. The Messianic mission that he began amid such extreme joy and high hopes has withered to nothingness. One of his closest friends has betrayed him, and the others misunderstand him. The masses praise him, but they do not follow him.

"Have I failed?" he asks. "Have you abandoned me because I failed you?"

His joyous baptism seems so long ago. Was it just a self-serving illusion? Was all that followed just a cruel hoax on those who believe in him?

The cheers of the multitudes that once rang so loudly in his ears are muted now. The memory seems so thin, so hollow, so useless. He wants to run as far away as he can and forget everything that has happened, go to a place where no one knows his name and live out his life in anonymity, perhaps become a carpenter and stone mason again like his father.

He lies flat on the ground, face down, and as the prospect of the cross imposes itself on him once again, he pleads again, "Father, I don't want to die. Not like this. All things are possible for you. Please remove this cup from me!"

He presses his forehead to the ground and the sweat and tears from his face pour into the earth. He takes a deep breath, summons all the courage within him, and says aloud and firmly, but very quietly: "But your will, not my will, be done!"

After a few moments of silence, he stands up, brushes himself off, returns to the spot where he left Peter, James and John — and finds them asleep. He shakes Peter awake.

"Peter, could you not stay awake one hour? Stay awake and pray that your mettle is not tested. Your spirit may be willing, but your flesh is weak."

James and John fumble awake as Yeshua returns to his solitary place. And there he fervently prays the same prayer.

"Please, Father, spare me the cross. Even if I have failed you, surely I've done nothing to deserve the cross. I've done everything I can to love you, and to teach and demonstrate that love. Why must I endure such agony and degradation? Please, Father, let me live."

He reasons. He pleads. But he ends his prayer with the same words he had used earlier in the night, speaking them from deep within his soul. "But your will, not my will, be done."

Then he returns to Peter, John, and James a second time — and finds them asleep again. He shakes them awake and all three are too humiliated with themselves to do more than mumble apologies. Yeshua says nothing to them, but instead returns to his solitude again, prays the same prayer again, returns to his friends again — and finds them sleeping a third time.

"Are you still sleeping?" he asks in amazement, not trying to mask his chagrin. "Enough!"

As the three stumble to their feet Yeshua motions them to be still. He listens intently for a moment, then his shoulders slightly slump.

"It is time," he says quietly. "My betrayer has come."

As he speaks, a detachment of men armed with swords and clubs marches out of the night. They quickly surround Yeshua and his three friends. In the dim moonlight, Yeshua recognizes some as temple guards and others as agents of the three sections of the Sanhedrin: chief priests, scribes and elders. At the head of the column is his disciple and friend, Judas. As the armed men watch menacingly, Judas walks directly to Yeshua and looks him in the eye.

"Teacher," he says.

He flings his arms around Yeshua's neck, jerks his head forward, and kisses him quickly and passionately on his mouth.

Judas withdraws and the armed men move in, heeding the pre-arranged signal that assures they don't make a mistake in the darkness and arrest the wrong man. As the mob grabs Yeshua, Peter grabs a sword and lays its blade hard against the head of one of the high priest's slaves. Blood starts to flow. The armed men start to turn on Peter, but Yeshua intervenes.

"Stop it!" he thunders over the commotion. His commanding voice momentarily shocks the mob into silence. "Those who live by the sword shall die by the sword! Peter! Put away the sword!"

As Peter drops the sword, a hush falls over the group and Yeshua hears the distant sound of men running. He knows the eight disciples he left near the road are running away in fear, but he ignores their retreating footsteps and directs his anger at the mob.

"You bring swords and clubs here to arrest me as though I were a criminal," he seethes. "Every day this week I was in the temple teaching and you could have arrested me at any time, but you didn't."

Suddenly, a peacefulness descends on Yeshua. He cannot understand it, cannot identify its source. Everything should feel wrong, but everything feels right. One of his disciples has betrayed him, eight others have deserted him, and the remaining three — his closest friends Peter, John, and James — are at this moment backing slowly away as they, too, prepare to desert him to save themselves. The throngs praise him, but do not follow him.

Yeshua is completely alone and in the hands of those who hate him the most. Soon, very soon, he will face the cruelest of punishments. He can almost feel the dreaded spikes in his wrists.

And yet, he feels more at peace and in control of his life than he ever has.

"But let the Scriptures be fulfilled," he says as he calmly holds out his hands for the guards to bind.

As two guards bind his hands behind him with course rope, Yeshua begins to smile. At first it's a faint smile, but as the guards surround him and shove him to start walking toward Jerusalem, the smile grows steadily into a broad grin. Despite his certainty now that the cross lies ahead he feels free, even joyous, and in complete control of his life. He laughs aloud at the thought that he could control anything while a mob marches him inexorably toward an agonizing death, but he knows it's true. Somehow, he has won. Without offering any defense, he has taken absolute love into the teeth of absolute evil, and defeated it.

Yeshua laughs again, this time because he realizes he has no idea how he, while being led to slaughter, has defeated anything, just that he has. Every indication says he failed, but he is certain he has succeeded.

Nothing makes sense, but everything makes sense. He is bound, but he is free. He is walking toward death, but he is striding toward life. He faces the most agonizing torture mankind has ever conceived, but he is joyous. This should be the worst moment of his life, but it is his best.

The physical, mental and spiritual duress that has plagued him over the last few weeks, days, and, especially, the last few hours, evaporates. He has not failed! His purpose was to reveal the one true God, and he has done that. He is with God now, and God is with him. He laughs again. A guard tells him to be quiet.

12

Covering themselves with darkness, and hiding Yeshua from the public by crowding closely around him, the Sanhedrin's mob moves quickly and quietly into Jerusalem. They head straight for Caiaphas' house.

Peter follows at a discreet distance. He is alone. John and James have joined the other disciples' flight. Although Peter knows he might be killed if he is recognized, he cannot abandon his friend and leader. He follows as closely as he dares. When the entourage reaches the high priest's house and goes inside, Peter melts into a crowd of guards who are warming themselves by a fire in the courtyard. There he waits to see what happens.

Inside the house, Yeshua is led into a large room where Caiaphas is sitting with the seventy chief priests, Sadducees, Pharisees, scribes, and elders who together form the Sanhedrin.

They are seated in a semicircle with Caiaphas in the center. Facing him is a single, straight-back chair, and several feet behind the chair is a row of chairs normally reserved for the rabbis' students, but empty tonight. The guards force Yeshua to sit in the lone chair. He recognizes the setting as that of a trial, and he knows he is the defendant.

As the Sanhedrin members settle into their seats, Yeshua feels a hand on his shoulder. He looks around to see the lawyer/scribe who had asked him a day earlier what the greatest commandment is.

"I want to help you, Yeshua," he says grimly, "but I don't know what I can do. From the looks of things they've already convicted you. This trial is illegal. It's a sham, a farce."

He kneels beside Yeshua so Yeshua can hear him better. "First, it's taking place in the high priest's house, which is illegal. The regulations governing the Sanhedrin, as spelled out in the *Mishnah*, specifically stipulate that all the Sanhedrin's decisions must be made in the temple's Hewn Stone Room. Any decision reached anywhere else is, by law, invalid.

"Second, this so-called trial is being held in the middle of the night, and that's another violation. The *Mishnah* regulation says all meetings of the Sanhedrin must be held during daylight hours.

"And third, the trial is being held during the Passover season, the most important festival in all Judaism, despite yet another *Mishnah* regulation that prohibits the Sanhedrin from meeting for any reason during any festival. I've tried to talk to Caiaphas about these violations, but he won't listen."

Caiaphas interrupts from his chair to inform Yeshua that he is accused of blasphemy. When Yeshua says nothing, Caiaphas calls his first witness. Before the witness can move the lawyer is on his feet again protesting.

"No!" he shouts. "The *Mishnah* regulations require that all criminal trials begin with a presentation that favors the accused's innocence. We demand — "

"Oh, sit down!" Caiaphas interrupts, brushing away the protest. A light laughter rolls through the room as Caiaphas motions for his first witness to come forth.

"I understand you heard Yeshua say he is the Messiah," Caiaphas asks the man. "Is that true?"

"Yes, sir. He was teaching in the temple and he said, 'I am the Messiah.' Just like that."

Caiaphas smiles at Yeshua as he tells the witness to be seated. He calls another witness, and another. He calls a whole parade of witnesses. They all testify the same thing: They heard Yeshua say he was the Messiah.

When Yeshua's defender has a chance to question the witnesses, he presses them for details. Under his questioning, their stories dissolve. Although all of them insist Yeshua claimed to be the Messiah, no two of them can agree on any of the details. Times, dates, places, circumstances — all the witnesses give different testimony.

When the last one leaves the stand the lawyer leans over to Yeshua and whispers, "Their testimony is worthless. The law says that in order for testimony to be accepted as valid, the testimonies of at least two witnesses must agree in detail. Since none of them agrees on any detail, their testimonies must be thrown out."

He turns his attention back to the floor as the witnesses file out. Then, above the mutterings of the Sanhedrin, he adds to Yeshua, "Apparently, these were all witnesses Caiaphas found on his own and got them to lie for him, so really all of them should be charged with perjury. Perjury is a capital offense when committed during a capital case, yet there they all go free."

Yeshua watches the witnesses walk out, but he says nothing. Caiaphas is chagrined by the setback, but far from being defeated.

"Don't worry," he assures the chief priest sitting next to him. "The next witnesses will convict him for certain. They'll testify that Yeshua healed them of a wide array of illnesses and maladies. Since only God can heal, it will prove that Yeshua claims to be God. We'll have him exactly where we want him."

"How do you know they're not lying, too?"

"Judas brought them to us. He swears they will tell the truth and Yeshua cannot deny any of it."

The priests turn their attention back to the trial as the second parade of witnesses begins testifying exactly what Caiaphas wants to hear.

"I was a paralytic and he told me to take up my bed and walk, and I did," one man testifies.

"My little girl died," another says. "Yeshua touched her and she became whole again."

"I had been suffering from hemorrhages for twelve years," a woman testifies, "I felt that if I could just touch his clothing I would be healed. I did touch his clothing one day, and I was healed."

"Demons used to possess me," a man says. "I would do all sorts of wild things. But Yeshua ordered the demons to leave me alone and they did. I haven't suffered that way since."

"I suffered seizures until Yeshua ordered the demons to leave me," a boy testifies. "And they did leave me. I haven't had a seizure since."

The witnesses continue to come, one after another, all eager to testify of their miraculous healings after Yeshua touched them. Caiaphas and his cohorts sit back, thoroughly enjoying the irrefutable evidence building to prove Yeshua's blasphemy.

When Yeshua's defender presses them for details, their stories do not change and it is clear they all are telling the truth. However, the value of their testimony melts to nothing.

"Well, he did tell me to take up my bed and walk, and I did. But he never specifically told me *he* healed me. He never really said who did."

"No, he never actually said *he* brought my little girl back to life. His words were that she was sleeping."

"Well, the hemorrhages did stop after I touched his clothing. But no, he didn't say *he* healed me. What he said was that my faith had made me whole."

"Yes, he ordered my demons to leave and they left. But he didn't say where his authority came from."

"That's what happened with my seizures."

Caiaphas' smugness vanishes bit by bit as it becomes apparent that none of the witnesses will testify that Yeshua ever claimed or accepted any credit for himself.

"This testimony is as useless as the perjurers'," a priest whispers nervously to Caiaphas. "What can we do?"

"We still have two other witnesses," Caiaphas snaps back. Then he shouts to a guard, "Bring the last two witnesses in here."

The final two witnesses swear they had heard Yeshua say, "I will destroy this temple that is made with hands, and in three days I will build another not made with hands." They don't agree on all the details, but their stories mesh well enough to make it plain to everyone that they are telling the truth.

Caiaphas glares at Yeshua. "Well? Have you no answer?"

Yeshua remains silent.

"What is it they testify against you?"

Yeshua remains silent.

Caiaphas runs out of patience. "I put you under the oath before the living God!" he erupts. "Tell us if you are the Messiah, the Son of God!"

The lawyer next to Yeshua leaps instantly to his feet.

"You can't ask that!" he protests. "That's a leading question, and the regulations prohibit leading questions because they could incriminate the witness if he answers them. You cannot ask that! It's illegal."

Caiaphas shifts his scornful glare from Yeshua to the lawyer.

"You've heard the proof," Caiaphas growls. "Let him answer if he can."

The lawyer spins to face Yeshua. "Don't answer," he demands. "You do not have to answer. If you decline to answer, the trial is over and you win. You go free. They've presented no credible witnesses against you, and they haven't presented one shred of evidence that could convict you. Remain silent and you'll walk out of here a free man."

"Answer me, Yeshua!" Caiaphas commands. "Are you the Messiah?"

Yeshua remains seated as he speaks for the first time since the trial began.

"That is what you have named me," he says in a strong yet relaxed voice that belies his fatigue.

"But I tell you," he continues, his voice rising, "from now on, you will see the Son of Man seated at the right hand of the power and coming on the clouds of heaven."

The room explodes in fury.

"He admits it!" a Pharisee shrieks. "He calls himself Son of Man! He called himself that when we were in Galilee, too. He's claiming he's the Messiah!"

"Yes," exhorts another. "And he said the words 'the power' and 'the clouds of heaven' — that proves it! He's talking about Daniel's vision of the Messiah's triumph and kingship. He is calling himself the Messiah!"

Caiaphas leaps to his feet and rips his clothes in mock horror. Finally, he has what he needs.

"Why do we still need witnesses?" he demands to his seventy colleagues. "You have heard his blasphemy! What is your decision?"

"Crucify him!" the Sanhedrin members roar back. "Kill him!"

"So be it!" Caiaphas roars in return, fully confident of his ability to get Rome to do that which it will not allow the Sanhedrin to do.

As the room explodes into pandemonium, the defense lawyer shouts in protest, but his words are lost in the commotion as many of the almost-delirious Sanhedrin members lunge for Yeshua and start shoving him and beating him with their fists.

The lawyer fights his way to Caiaphas and pleads desperately, "Please! Stop this! At least follow the Law! If they don't give their verdict one at a time, starting with the youngest and ending with the oldest, the verdict is invalid. That is the Law!"

Caiaphas only laughs in reply. "Yeshua is a blasphemer and he's going to die," he grunts.

"Then at least delay it for one day," the lawyer pleads. "The Law demands it. Even before Rome suspended our right to administer capital punishment, the Law stipulated that at least one night pass before it can be carried out. At least give him that. Don't have a man killed in the heat of the moment. Please!"

But Caiaphas only waves him away and happily turns his attention back to the scene before him. The lawyer slumps into his chair in full defeat, staring dully and helplessly at the same scene. The jeering mob has blindfolded Yeshua now and someone hits him in the face with his fist.

"Can you tell who hit you?" he mocks, and the mob hoots gleefully when Yeshua does not answer. Instead, they pound him with their fists until blood begins to pour from his nose and he falls to the floor.

"Prophesy!" they yell at him, howling with laughter as they kick him and spit on him.

Caiaphas lets the cacophony go on for awhile as he watches with amusement, then orders the guards to take charge of Yeshua.

"Hold him until we call for him, probably a little after dawn."

As the guards wrest control of Yeshua from the mob and lead him away, Caiaphas settles his colleagues. "This session of the Sanhedrin is adjourned," he announces. "At dawn we'll reconvene briefly in the temple to formalize the conviction."

As the members begin to file out, Caiaphas says privately to the priest, "Technically, voting in the temple during daylight hours won't make Yeshua's conviction legal — we may have taken too many shortcuts for that. But it will be enough to get our case before Rome's appointed governor here."

"Pontius Pilate? You're sure?"

"Absolutely. Pilate's job is to keep peace in Palestine, and when we show Pilate that Yeshua is guilty of treason against Rome, he'll order Yeshua executed on the spot. Pilate won't care about legal technicalities."

He smiles at the priest. The priest smiles back.

"And there'll be peace again in the temple," the priest says. "Life will return to normal."

"Exactly!"

13

eter stands by the fire outside Caiaphas' house as he awaits some word of Yeshua's fate. A servant girl of the high priest walks by and glimpses his face in the firelight. She thinks she recognizes him. She stops and stares at him for a long moment until she feels sure she does.

"You were with that man from Nazareth," she says, accusation dripping from each word.

"I don't know what you're talking about," Peter replies.

The woman looks at him dubiously, but she leaves without saying anything further. Peter, knowing he could be killed if he is revealed as Yeshua's top lieutenant, moves away from the firelight. Nevertheless, despite his fear, he refuses to abandon his friend inside the building. Instead, he takes up a new position at the gate where there is less light, making it harder for anyone to identify him.

The servant girl had not been persuaded by Peter's denial. Later, she searches him out and examines his face closely. It convinces her more than ever that she is right.

"You are one of them!" she blurts.

"I am not!" Peter fires back, stalking away to another part of the courtyard. He is more frightened than ever, but still determined not to leave Yeshua alone.

The servant girl will not be put off. She persuades several bystanders in the area to find him again and confirm her suspicions. One of the bystanders tries to strike up a conversation with him. As soon as Peter says a word, the man's eyes widen.

"You're a Galilean; I can tell from your accent," he says with amazement. "You *were* with the Nazarene!"

This time Peter curses loudly.

"Listen!" he retorts, hoping the fear in his voice sounds like anger, "I swear to you! I do not know the man you're talking about!"

At that moment, Peter hears a bugle sound in the distance, signaling the Roman guard's three o'clock changing. He freezes in horror as he remembers that the Romans call the bugle blow the *gallicinium* — the cockcrow. The words Yeshua had spoken to him only a few hours earlier come flooding back.

"Peter," he had said sadly, "this night, before the cock crows twice, you will deny me three times."

Peter sinks to his knees and breaks down in great sobs. Tears pour down his face. Judas had betrayed Yeshua. The other disciples had abandoned him. Now, even Peter has denied him.

At the lowest moment of Yeshua's life, every one of his closest friends has deserted him, leaving him entirely alone, just as Yeshua said they would.

Peter is still weeping at dawn when he sees the guards lead Yeshua away from Caiaphas' house and take him to the temple.

צ צ צ צ

Judas also watches Yeshua being led away. Because Judas helped the Sanhedrin trap Yeshua, Caiaphas let him watch the trial. And what Judas saw enraged him. It was not at all what he had planned. He intended to force Yeshua to declare his Messiahship, bring down the wrath of God on the evil that had taken control of the temple, lead the Jews to a magnificent victory over the hated Rome, and restore all power to Jews. But Yeshua is not supposed to die. Judas doesn't hate Yeshua; he loves him. He had only wanted to force Yeshua's hand, not kill him. When he saw the Sanhedrin condemn Yeshua he realized that was exactly what he had done.

He had not been able to get to the chief priests during the trial. As soon as the trial ended, they headed for the temple so they could be there at dawn to formalize their decision. They are in the temple awaiting dawn when Judas catches up with them.

"I have betrayed innocent blood," he tells them.

The priests laugh at him.

"Why should we care?" one snarls. The others smirk their agreement.

"Please!" Judas cries, his eyes widening with desperation. "I've committed a terrible crime. I beg you, please reverse your decision. Yeshua is innocent! Let him go! I'll give you back all your silver."

But the priests only laugh scornfully at him. Judas reads the hatred in their eyes and realizes it is too late. In horrified shock, he begins to back away.

"He's dead!" he exclaims. "Yeshua is dead! I've killed him!"

"Yes," a chief priest replies. "Surely you knew this would happen."

The other Sanhedrin members laugh again. They enjoy watching Judas squirm helplessly in his misery. In frustration, Judas flings the silver down at the priests' feet and, streaming tears, runs blindly from the temple. He runs through the throngs of festival celebrants and out the Dung Gate.

He runs without knowing or caring where he's going. He runs until he can run no farther, then collapses onto the hard, rocky ground and writhes in agony. His heart is broken, and nothing will help him. He has murdered the best friend he's ever had, the best he could imagine having, and he can neither live with himself nor escape himself.

He lifts his head and realizes he is overlooking the Hinnom Valley, not far from its conjunction with the Kidron Valley — the "Valley of Fire," where Jerusalem burns its refuse. He can smell the stench of burning garbage and, as he looks toward the fires, he knows what he will do. He rises slowly and deliberately to his feet and moves mechanically toward the valley. When he sees the fires, he leaves the road, stumbling and sliding down the steep, rocky, nearly lifeless hillside.

Near its base, within sight of the burning garbage, he finds a sturdy tree, tall enough for his purpose. He climbs the tree, ties one end of his belt to a limb, loops the other end around his neck, and pushes himself off.

א א א א

As soon as Caiaphas can see the sun, the Sanhedrin formalizes its decision to have Yeshua killed. Caiaphas orders the guards to bring Yeshua to the temple. As soon as the prisoner arrives, the Sanhedrin rises as one and, ignoring Yeshua, moves en masse toward the door. Caiaphas tells the guards to follow them, and together they lead the bound, bruised, and bleeding Yeshua to the Fortress of Antonio, which adjoins the temple's northern wall. There Pontius Pilate, who is just waking up, appears on the front steps. Caiaphas wastes no time.

"We have convicted this man, this Yeshua, of blasphemy. That merits death by stoning under our Law, but our Law, of course, is suspended. Be that as it may, this man also has violated Roman law. He is a revolutionary. He subverts the people, incites them to refuse to pay their taxes to Caesar, and claims to be a king — all capital offenses against Rome. We therefore demand that you, as governor of Palestine, have him crucified immediately. Today!"

Pilate rubs his eyes and, ignoring Yeshua, speaks directly to Caiaphas.

"Even if your charges are true," he says, "doesn't your law also say twenty-four hours must pass between a capital conviction and execution?"

Caiaphas frowns. Postponing Yeshua's death is out of the question because if Yeshua isn't on the cross today, his followers will realize what's happening. An angry mob would form. A riot would follow.

Caiaphas thinks quickly. "A mere technicality," he replies cooly. "The truth is that this man is guilty of sedition against Rome. He has committed capital crimes against Rome and he does not deserve to live. He must be executed today."

"He claims to be king," a chief priest yells at Pilate. "That's a crime against Rome. Crucify him!"

Pilate senses the crowd's charged emotional state and plays for time. He looks closely at the man they accuse. Dried blood streaks his face and spatters his clothing. Yet, his face reflects calmness and dignity. His eyes are fixed on the horizon, and there is a hint of a smile.

"I'm very pleased to meet you, Yeshua," Pilate says. "I've heard about you. I'm fascinated by what I've heard."

He waits for a reaction. When Yeshua says nothing, he continues. "Look at you! Twelve months ago you were an itinerant religious teacher, an unknown — a nobody! And yet, when you arrived in Jerusalem last Sunday, the rabble greeted you as if you were their king."

He emphasizes the word 'king' and pauses to see Yeshua's reaction. When Yeshua still says nothing, Pilate continues. "Many Jews seem to think their God has specifically chosen you to save them. Are you God, Yeshua? Are you going to save them?"

Still no reply.

"I have to admire you, Yeshua. I've heard how you delighted the rabble by causing that ruckus in the temple. You humiliated your leaders, but you thrilled the rabble. You're a growing legend, Yeshua. Tell me, are you king of the Jews?"

Yeshua breaks his silence by speaking out boldly and loudly.

"That is what you have named me!"

The chief priests erupt into a babble of jeering shouts and accusations. Pilate waves them silent and speaks again to Yeshua. "You hear their accusations," he says. "Don't you have an answer?"

Yeshua says nothing.

"You amaze me, Yeshua. With one word, I can have you crucified — a horrible way to die — or I can set you free. I am your only hope, Yeshua. You know that. Yet, you won't defend yourself. And you seem so calm, so peaceful, so in control. Why?" His voice is earnest, thoughtful. Yeshua does not answer.

As Pilate gazes at him, he sees his wife at the top of the

steps, motioning frantically to get his attention. The unusualness and apparent urgency of her presence in the midst of official business surprises him, but it also provides him an opportunity to back away for a moment and organize his thoughts.

He leaves Yeshua on the steps and climbs to the porch where his wife, standing with several of Pilate's advisers, anxiously awaits him.

"You can't have him crucified!" she exclaims. "I had a vision last night. This man is innocent! Please, wash your hands of him! Have nothing to do with him. I beg you!"

Pilate is amused. "I have no intention of crucifying him," he says. "He's as innocent as you are of committing crimes against Rome. I know that. And I don't crucify innocent people! If Caiaphas thinks I'm going to believe his lies, he's a fool."

Satisfied, Pilate's wife smiles her gratitude and returns inside the fortress. Pilate confers with his advisers before he goes back to the Sanhedrin.

"This is a curious man. As far as he knows I'm about to have him nailed to a cross, and yet he won't defend himself and he remains so peaceful. I don't understand that. I respect it, but I don't understand it."

"You sound as if you like the man."

Pilate winces. "Like him? Of course I don't like him. He's a Jew, and how can anybody like a Jew? Their superstitions are beyond reason, and they're fanatical about them. No, I don't like him. I really don't care whether he lives or dies."

"It might be well to let him die, then," another adviser says as he studies faces in the crowd. "Look at those men. I've never seen such hatred! Since Yeshua means nothing to us, I say let the Sanhedrin have its way."

"Hear me!" Pilate flashes back, anger and finality in his voice. "Caesar appointed me governor here because I served him well in many positions, civilian and military. For me to condemn any man I know is innocent would be to commit murder, and that would betray the impartial justice that is the glory of Rome. It would betray Caesar himself! And that, my friends, I swear to you, I will never do!"

"Yeshua must have done something severe for the Sanhedrin to be this angry," the adviser persists.

"Oh, I'm sure he violated some of their stupid little superstitions, but that's their problem, not mine. And it certainly isn't Rome's. If the Jews have a problem with Yeshua, they'll have to deal with it."

Pilate descends the steps again, but as he approaches Yeshua, he speaks directly to the Sanhedrin. "I find this man innocent of your charges," he announces.

The Sanhedrin erupts in angry disbelief.

"He's been causing trouble ever since he started teaching and preaching in Galilee," Caiaphas yells over the din.

"Galilee?" Pilate says, his eyebrows rising with inspiration. "He's from Galilee?"

"Yes."

"Well, then," Pilate says, rubbing his hands together and grinning with relief. "If he's a Galilean, he's under Herod Antipas' jurisdiction. This is Herod's problem, not mine. Herod is in Jerusalem now for your Passover. He's in his palace right now. Take this man to Herod. Let Herod decide."

Caiaphas orders the guards to close ranks tightly around Yeshua so no one in the streets will be able to identify him, and they hurry him to Herod's palace on Jerusalem's west side.

"This is even better," Caiaphas confides to a chief priest as they leave the Fort of Antonio. "Herod has no use for Yeshua or his family. Yeshua is as good as dead."

The walk takes fewer than ten minutes. When they arrive, Herod Antipas is delighted to see Yeshua. All his life he's heard intriguing stories about Yeshua, and in recent weeks the Herodians have been telling him even more incredible tales. Herod is especially curious about the reports that Yeshua can heal the sick simply by touching them.

"I've heard a lot about you, Yeshua," Herod says coldly. "I've been hoping to see you perform some sign."

When Yeshua does not respond, Herod glares down on him with contempt. "This filthy, bruised, bleeding creature is a king?" Herod laughs, looking in the direction of Caiaphas.

Caiaphas laughs too, but says nothing.

Turning his attention back to Yeshua, Herod pummels him with contemptuous questions. "Are you a king? Why are you bleeding and bruised if you are a king? Where is your kingdom?" The Sanhedrin's agents join in by ridiculing him and hurling accusations of their own at him.

Still Yeshua says nothing, and the silence infuriates Herod.

"Guards," he shouts, pointing at Yeshua, "this person is a king. A king should have a robe. Give him a robe."

The guards, laughing at Herod's sarcasm, drape an elegant robe around Yeshua's shoulders. With a sweeping flourish, Herod bows deeply and, with all the sarcasm he can muster, says, "Your Majesty."

His guards and the temple officials howl with laughter, "Hail to the king!" they shout, laughing uproariously.

"Long live the king!"

Yeshua stands still, says nothing.

Soon Herod tires of his amusement. Leaving the kingly robe draped around Yeshua's shoulders as a parting gesture of contempt, Herod laughs at him one more time and orders that he be sent back to Pilate.

"If Pilate wants to crucify him," he tells the Sanhedrin delegation, "I don't care."

Pilate, still standing on the Fortress of Antonio porch, looks out to see the crowd bringing Yeshua back to him. He curses.

"I hoped I'd never have to see that man again," he mutters to an adviser. "Herod should have handled this!"

"But Herod didn't handle it. You'll have to. What are you going to do?"

"Yeshua is innocent; I'll set him free, of course. It's just that if the Sanhedrin wants him crucified as badly as it seems to, they might cause trouble."

The adviser raises his eyebrows, but says nothing. Pilate sighs.

"I'm vulnerable to blackmail," he finally says. "Though it's true I've served Caesar well during most of my years in government, I made two critical mistakes in Palestine. If the Sanhedrin were to formally report either of them to Rome, Caesar would remove me as governor of Palestine and I would go home in disgrace. Everything I've worked for would be destroyed."

The adviser remains silent. There is nothing to say. He knows Pilate's mistakes, and he knows Pilate's assessment of them is accurate.

The first mistake stemmed from what Pilate considered the Jews' irrational religious fanaticism. Roman troops marched under a standard topped by the emperor's image, but because the emperor was officially a god, and Jewish law forbade images of God, governors customarily appeased the Jews by removing the image whenever their troops marched into Jerusalem. When Pilate became governor, he refused to follow the custom. Instead, he ordered his troops to march into Jerusalem with the images in place. The Jews revolted by demonstrating in the streets, and when they were still demonstrating six days later, Pilate ordered his troops to surround the protesters and draw their swords.

Once the Jews were corralled, he told them he would have them all killed immediately if they did not stop demonstrating. The Jews threw themselves onto the ground and bared their necks, signaling they would gladly accept death rather than let the wisdom of their Law be transgressed. Pilate backed down.

Pilate's second mistake actually began as a good idea. He proposed to build a new water supply system for Jerusalem, financing it with temple funds. The Jews wanted the new system, but they rebelled at using temple funds to pay for it. Pilate insisted. Many Jews revolted by again demonstrating in the streets. Pilate ordered them to disband. When they refused, Pilate ordered his troops to hide bludgeons under their cloaks and, on a given signal, attack the protesters and disburse them. The soldiers overreacted and, when the ensuing melee ended, a number of Jews lay dead in the streets.

Caiaphas' arrival at the Fortress of Antonio's steps with Yeshua interrupts the Roman officials' thoughts and demands their full attention. As Caiaphas reports on the events at Herod's palace, Pilate studies the battered, bleeding Yeshua. He takes special note of the robe, knowing that Herod doesn't care whether Yeshua lives or dies. Pilate is on his own.

When Caiaphas finishes his report, Pilate turns to the crowd and announces, "I find this man innocent of any wrongdoing."

The crowd erupts in fury. "Crucify him!" they shout. "Kill him!"

Pilate waves them to silence. "You have brought me a man you say is seducing Jews from their allegiance to Rome. I have examined him in your presence and I can find nothing in him to condemn, certainly nothing that merits crucifixion. Neither did Herod, or he wouldn't have sent him back to me. I will therefore have Yeshua flogged and release him to you. If he has broken any of your laws, you can handle that yourselves."

The crowd roars back with louder and more intense anger. "No!" they shriek. "Crucify him! Crucify him!"

"Pontius Pilate!" Caiaphas bellows over the roar. "If you don't crucify Yeshua, you are no friend of Caesar!"

The words cut into Pilate like cold daggers. Blood rushes away from his face, and his skin feels damp and cold as he interprets Caiaphas' words — accurately — as the blackmail Pilate fears the most. He feels faint as he realizes his only options may be to murder an innocent man or to see his long and distinguished career crumble in disgrace.

Pilate fights back panic as he searches for some other option. He needs time. He motions to Caiaphas to give him a moment, then starts to climb the steps to the porch where his advisers still stand. As he does, he glances at the crowd and it strikes him how much it has grown since the Sanhedrin and Yeshua had arrived at dawn. The newcomers are clamoring for him to exercise his custom of letting one prisoner go free in honor of Passover. Pilate ruefully wishes he could free Yeshua and be done with it, but he knows that is impossible.

Or is it?

Pilate darts up the steps and grabs his adviser's shoulder. "I have an idea," he says, urgency mixing with hope in his voice. "You know how much the rabble loves Yeshua. They've been clamoring after him all week. If I give them a choice between freeing Yeshua or some common criminal, surely they'll choose Yeshua. They're a rabid bunch. They'll drown out the Sanhedrin's protests and I'll have no choice but to let Yeshua go."

"It might work," the adviser says, rubbing his chin. "But who?"

"There's a prisoner named Barabbas in the dungeon. He's ideal."

"Who is he?"

"He's a common thief who got involved with a murder during a street uprising. Given a choice between freeing a murderer and an innocent man, whom they adore, surely the crowd will free the innocent man. Get Barabbas out here fast!"

When a surprised, confused Barabbas arrives from the dungeon, Pilate marches him and Yeshua to the top of the steps. He stands between them and calls out to the crowd:

"Whom shall I release? Yeshua the king of the Jews, or Barabbas the murderer?"

"Barabbas," the crowd roars back in unison, the new arrivals screaming just as loudly as the temple rulers. "Free Barabbas!"

Pilate is stunned. He turns to his advisers. "Why aren't they calling for Yeshua's release?" he asks in dismay. "All week they've been praising Yeshua like he was their king, even their God. Now they want him dead. What happened?"

His advisers return blank looks. They're as surprised as he is. Pilate looks back to the crowd and signals them to be quiet so he can speak.

"But what about Yeshua?" he asks. "What shall I do with this man you call your Messiah?"

"Crucify him," the crowd screams gleefully. "Crucify him!"

"But what evil has he done? Barabbas is a murderer, but what has Yeshua done? I have examined him, and I find nothing to condemn. What about Yeshua?"

"Crucify him!" the crowd roars, louder and more insistent than ever. "Crucify him! Free Barabbas."

Pilate slumps as, too late, he realizes what has happened. Yeshua had been arrested, tried, convicted and sentenced during the night, in secret, while the Passover Festival celebrants slept. Now the celebrants are just waking up and beginning to prepare for the day. They don't even know Yeshua has been arrested, much less that the Sanhedrin has tried, convicted and sentenced him to die. If they knew, they would be pouring into the streets to save him. But they're not here. The mob that joined the Sanhedrin in the street is composed of Barabbas' friends who know Barabbas has been convicted and, knowing the governor's custom of releasing a prisoner at Passover, have come to secure his release. All they want is Barabbas' freedom. They don't care what happens to Yeshua.

"Crucify him!" the crowd roars. "Kill him!"

Sweat rolls down Pilate's face and neck. He wishes he had stayed at his permanent headquarters in Caesarea instead of coming to Jerusalem to witness the feast of Passover. If he were in Caesarea, he wouldn't be faced with this decision. But he is here, and he has to decide.

The crowd's screams fill his senses. He feels the Sanhedrin members' hatred for Yeshua, and the newcomers' rabid support for Barabbas. None will be placated. He looks at Yeshua, still standing motionless on the steps. He thinks of his career. He is alone in an angry mob. It is too much to handle. He gives up. He turns to Yeshua.

"Why should I help you, Yeshua?" he exhorts in frustration. "You won't even help yourself, so why should I help you? I've done all I can for you, Yeshua. There's nothing more I can do."

The mob goes delirious with the taste of victory as Pilate pours water into a bowl and makes a great show of washing his hands. When he finishes, he holds up his clean hands for everyone to see, and yells to them: "I am innocent of the blood of this just man! The blood for this will be on your hands, not mine!"

In its delirium, the mob doesn't care. Some are elated that Barabbas is to be freed, some ecstatic that Yeshua will be crucified. Either way, everyone is jubilant.

"Let the blood be on us and our children," they scream back exultantly.

Pilate feels miserable as he turns to the soldiers. "Release Barabbas," he orders. "Prepare Yeshua for crucifixion."

The soldiers untie the ropes that hold Barabbas and release him. Then they begin the routine that precedes all crucifixions. They strip Yeshua naked, bind his hands tightly behind his back, bend him over double so that his back is exposed at just the right angle for a flogging, and tie him to a post.

A soldier appears with a scourge specifically designed for pre-crucifixion floggings. It is a long leather thong studded with bits of bone and sharpened pieces of lead, intended to shred the flesh off a prisoner's back, leaving it in ribbons.

Sometimes the flogging rips out a prisoner's eyes. Sometimes it kills the victim before he gets to the cross. Very seldom does a victim remain conscious through it.

The soldier leans back and puts all his strength into bringing the whip down hard on Yeshua's back. He lashes him again, and again, and again. Thirty-nine times he slashes the whip across Yeshua's back.

When it ends, Yeshua's back is shredded, but he is still conscious. Pilate methodically continues with the pre-crucifixion routine by reciting the prescribed words for all to hear.

"Illum duci ad crucem placet," he says. "The sentence is that this man should be taken to a cross."

Then, without pausing, he turns to a Roman soldier. *"I, miles, expedi crucem.* Go, soldier, and prepare the cross."

A detachment of four soldiers marches off immediately to begin preparing the cross' horizontal beam. They will force Yeshua to carry it through the streets to the place of his execution just outside Jerusalem's northwestern wall. Under normal circumstances they would make him carry the crossbeam naked, but as a concession to the Jews, who consider public nakedness a disgrace, they put Yeshua's clothes back on him and take him to their barracks.

While they wait, Pilate's bodyguards join them and, taking a cue from Herod and his guards, drape a purple robe over Yeshua as a mocking symbol of kingship. One bodyguard forces a reed into his right hand and makes him hold it as a king would hold a scepter. Another fashions a king's crown out of thorns and jams it down so hard on Yeshua's head that the thorns cut deeply into his scalp and send streams of blood flowing down over his face and neck.

"Hail! King of the Jews!" the guards and soldiers bellow at him, hooting at their bruised and bleeding captive. They fall to their knees in front of him in raucous homage. One of the soldiers strikes his head with a reed. Others spit on him.

When the cross' horizontal beam is ready, the soldiers quit their fun and return to the task at hand. They remove the purple robe and put Yeshua's own clothes back on him. Then they return him to Pilate.

Pilate has one last task to perform before the soldiers lead Yeshua away to be crucified. Routinely, before sending anyone to his crucifixion, Pilate writes that person's crime on a placard for the soldiers to carry to Golgotha. The lead soldier will carry the placard in front of him so as many bystanders as possible will see why the prisoner is being crucified.

Pilate writes the words in big, bold letters in three languages, Latin, Aramaic and Greek:

Yeshua of Nazareth
King of the Jews

As soon as the chief priests see the inscription, they vehemently object. "No," they shout. "Write 'blasphemy.'"

"No."

"Then write 'insurrectionist,'" they plead.

"No."

"At least write, 'He said I am king of the Jews,' not just 'King of the Jews.'"

Pilate refuses to yield.

"What I have written, I have written," he declares. "The subject is closed — permanently!"

Pilate turns his back to the priests and walks away, ignoring further protests. The Sanhedrin emissaries have no choice but to accept defeat.

"Let it go," Caiaphas orders. "It's a small enough price to pay."

They return their attention to the soldiers, who already have forced Yeshua to pick up the heavy wooden beam. He will carry it to the Place of the Skull, where it will be affixed to a post already at the site and become the crossbeam of the cross on which he will die.

Yeshua stands in the middle of a four-soldier, diamond-shaped formation. The soldier carrying the placard marches directly in front of Yeshua, two others march on his left and right, and the fourth follows close behind him.

The lead soldier takes a long route through Jerusalem's narrow streets so that the maximum possible number of people will see the spectacle and take warning.

Soon after they begin the march, though, Yeshua's strength fails and he collapses. The soldiers curse him, beat him, kick him, whip him. But he is too exhausted, too weak, too near death. He cannot pick up the crossbeam.

"Leave him be," the lead soldier finally orders. "We want him alive when we put him on the cross."

He looks into a group of bystanders and points at one strong-looking man.

"You," he orders, "pick up the crossbeam and carry it for him."

The man does as he is told. The soldiers pick up Yeshua and push him forward.

As the procession winds its way through Jerusalem's narrow stone alleys, the masses who had welcomed Yeshua to Jerusalem with such hope and joy only a few days earlier watch in silence. It was one thing to cheer him on in the temple as he took on the Pharisees and Sadducees, but it is another thing entirely to take on Rome. It was exciting and fun to be a nameless face in a crowd jeering the temple's corrupt establishment, but it would be suicide to try and stop Rome.

While most people watch in silence as the procession passes, a small group of men and women, mostly Galilean and Samaritan women, follow as closely as they dare. All are frightened. Most are weeping. None can bear to see Yeshua crucified, but none can stop it. All of them have had encounters with Yeshua that elevated them beyond what they could have imagined possible, and regenerated their hope. They will not desert him now.

14

The soldiers lead Yeshua out of Jerusalem through the Gennath Gate and take him to Golgotha, a gray, abandoned rock quarry northwest of the city where stones were once cut to build the temple. Locals call it the Place of the Skull because a hillside there resembles a skull, and also because Roman soldiers use it as their killing ground.

The soldiers uncaringly throw Yeshua onto the dusty quarry floor between two crosses where two men already have been crucified. Above each man's head is a placard that reads, "thief." The soldiers tell the man carrying Yeshua's crossbeam to throw it on the ground beside him. He does as he is told, vanishing as soon as he sees an opportunity. One soldier bends over Yeshua and pushes a wet sponge to his face.

"Drink it," he says. "It's spiced wine. It'll help numb the pain."

Yeshua motions that he doesn't want it. The soldier shrugs and tosses it away.

"I don't care whether you take it or not," he says. "We only have to offer it to appease the Jews." His voice suddenly becomes thick with exaggerated sarcasm. "The Jews are more humane than we are." The other soldiers snicker.

As they make their routine preparations, they ignore Yeshua, and he is thankful for the respite. He is exhausted. He hasn't slept in more than twenty-four hours. Insects swarm to his bleeding wounds. He is painfully thirsty; he's had nothing to drink since he drank wine at the Passover meal Thursday night, some twelve hours ago.

The soldier in charge of the detail picks up the placard upon which Pilate had written his verdict.

"Oh!" The soldier says in mock surprise and admiration, heavy with sarcasm. "This says you're 'King of the Jews.' You're a very important person, sir, so you deserve our very special treatment. We're going to hang you from a cross that's taller than the others."

His voice hardens as he continues. "That way all your Jew friends will see clearly what happens to important people, even kings like you, when they defy Rome."

The soldiers laugh as they obtain a long post, fit the crossbeam into a pre-cut notch in the top of the post to form a cross, and lay the cross face up on the ground. They install Pilate's placard so passers-by will be able to see who the criminal is and what crime he has committed.

Then they strip off all Yeshua's clothes and throw them in a heap on the ground. They roughly pick up his naked body, stretch him over the cross, and drive heavy spikes through his wrists so that his body's weight will rest on bone and not tear the flesh off his hands when they set the cross upright. Yeshua screams at the pain, but the soldiers ignore him.

"Nail or saddle?" one of the soldiers asks.

"Saddle," comes the reply.

The soldiers methodically attach the saddle to the cross' vertical post, straddle Yeshua's naked body on it, and jam him down on it so hard that a trickle of dark red blood spills from the corner of his mouth. They tie his feet together loosely to prevent them from flailing around, place the cross' vertical post in a socket in the ground, and stand the cross upright between the two thieves. When it locks into position in its socket, the soldiers stand back and look up at him.

"All we have to do now is wait 'til you're dead," one says.

With that, the soldiers begin rummaging through Yeshua's clothes to see if there is anything they can use for themselves. It is nine o'clock in the morning on Friday.

At first, Yeshua is aware only of the physical pain that saturates his body: the spikes through his wrists, the saddle between his legs, his whip-shredded back, the swarming insects, the thirst, the exhaustion. Blood, sweat, and grime cake his eyes.

He is still aware of his surroundings. His head droops forward and he sees the soldiers beneath him at the foot of his cross. They are dividing his clothes among them. One soldier takes his inner robe, one his girdle, a third his turban, a fourth his sandals. Four soldiers, five pieces of clothing.

The only piece remaining is the seamless coat his mother gave to him as he began his ministry. Recognizing its high quality, the soldiers decide not to ruin it by dividing it among themselves. Instead, as Yeshua watches them, they gamble for it.

As they draw lots, Yeshua becomes aware of raucous, ugly taunts being spit at him from not far away. He raises his head enough to see little knots of Pharisees, Sadducees, scribes, chief priests, and elders approaching him.

"You who're going to tear down the temple and rebuild it in three days, come down from there and save yourself!" a Sadducee yells at him. His friends laugh uproariously.

"Let this 'Messiah,' this 'King of the Jews,' come down from the cross so that we may all see and believe!" a Pharisee whoops. When Yeshua does not respond, they howl with more laughter.

A chief priest mocks him. "He saved others, but he can't save himself," he shouts, laughing.

Another cries: "He trusted God; now let God have him — *if* God wants him!"

Rolls of contemptuous laughter hit Yeshua's ears like hammers. He drops his head and looks again at the soldiers beneath his feet as they gamble for his last shred of clothing.

He feels profound sorrow for them. They are not evil, just ignorant. They are blind; they cannot see the sun shining into their eyes. They are not to be hated; they are to be pitied.

"Forgive them, Father," he says aloud. "They don't know what they're doing."

The taunts increase. They become louder and more vicious than ever.

Yeshua hears a hoarse, raspy voice come from the thief below him to his right.

"Are you not the anointed one of God?" he sneers through his pain. "Save yourself and us!"

"Stop it!" snaps the thief on Yeshua's left. His voice is as hoarse and pained as the first, but it is full of anger. "Don't you fear even God? You and I deserve to be here, but this man hasn't done anything!"

The thief drops his voice and speaks directly to Yeshua, the anger gone.

"Yeshua, please remember me when you come into your kingdom," he says.

Yeshua almost smiles.

"I tell you the truth," he says. "On this day, you will be with me in Paradise."

"Paradise!" The thief repeats the word in an awed whisper, astonished that Yeshua would use it. Paradise is a Persian word that literally translates as "walled garden," but Persians use it in a way that lifts it far beyond its literal translation. Whenever a Persian king wants to specially honor one of his subjects, he invites the subject to walk with him inside his paradise. The thief realizes Yeshua is offering him a very special place with God in eternity. He can speak no more.

As the morning wears on, the hecklers tire of throwing insults at a man who will not respond. They drift into the background and start chatting among themselves as they wait for him to die. Their only interest now is to verify his death, to make certain he does not somehow escape. As time slowly passes, most of the insults hurled at Yeshua come from passers-by.

The small knot of people who followed Yeshua to the quarry, most of them women, edge to the foot of Yeshua's cross. They know they can do nothing to help him and they risk great personal danger by publicly siding with him, but they draw near to him anyway. Yeshua's blurred vision prevents him from seeing them clearly, but he recognizes Mary, his mother; Salome, his mother's sister and mother of the disciples John and James; John, the only disciple he can see; and Mary Magdalene, who has loved Yeshua since she met him. He can see a few other people, but they're standing too far away for him to recognize.

Yeshua focuses his attention on his mother and John as they stand closely together.

"Mother, see your son," he croaks through his dust-dry throat. "John, see your mother."

Mary and John understand his words. Custom dictates that the oldest son in a family is responsible for the care of his widowed mother, and if he dies the next-oldest brother assumes the responsibility. But Yeshua knows his brothers are not ready to care for her; they haven't even accompanied her to this place.

John has, though. He is risking his life to stand with her. Yeshua is telling John to care for his mother.

Mary and John, both weeping, helpless to change the horror before them, turn and walk slowly away. The others, just as helpless, follow. There is nothing they can do.

The day continues to creep by. Noonday passes. The sun beats down relentlessly and the temperature pushes inexorably upward. Insects swarm. Yeshua gasps for air. He feels that God is an eternity away. Has God abandoned him?

But even as the thought strikes him, a favorite Psalm, the twenty-second, arises from the mist of his subconscious. He had thought of the Psalm many times over the last few days because it reminds him that God is always nearest in the most desperate and loneliest of times, even when — *especially* when — he seems farthest away. Although Yeshua feels his life slipping away, the words of the Psalm lift his spirits, and he senses the joy of touching the heart of God. He wants to shout the entire Psalm as loud as he can, but all he can manage is to croak out its first few words:

"My God, my God, why have you forsaken me?"

His voice breaks. He can speak no more. He marvels at how the Psalm's words speak so clearly to him at this particular moment.

Some bystanders who hear Yeshua's voice think he's calling for the prophet Elijah, and they began to taunt him anew. "Oh, let's see if Elijah will come and bring him down from the cross," they sing gleefully.

Though the Psalm brings comfort to Yeshua's soul, his body allows him no rest. His parched throat hurts from shouting out those few words. His swelling tongue crowds his mouth.

"I'm thirsty," he manages to say.

A soldier impales a sponge soaked in vinegar and lifts it up to Yeshua's mouth. Yeshua jerks his head away as the soldiers laugh.

He can take no more, and he has nothing more to give. It is over. A prayer from his childhood floats into his mind. It is a bedtime prayer that his mother had taught him when he was a child, just as countless Jewish mothers around the world and across many generations had taught their children. Yeshua repeats part of the prayer now, altering it from its original form only by preceding it with the word "father."

"Father," he whispers with his last bit of strength, "into your hands I commit my spirit."

Yeshua feels the last vestige of consciousness draining away. His breathing is erratic and painful, his energy gone.

Summoning every iota of energy still in him, he draws a deep breath, leans his head back as far as he can, and lets out one final, strong, victorious shout:

"It . . . is . . . *FINISHED!!*"

His head droops forward. His body becomes still, goes limp.

A Roman centurian who has been observing Yeshua hears his shout. He walks to the foot of the cross and looks up at the limp body hanging there. He stands quietly for a long time before he speaks.

"Truly," he says reverently, "this was a man of God."

For awhile, no one else notices that Yeshua is dead. Everyone is ignoring him. The soldiers are involved in a game. The Sanhedrin emissaries stand around in little knots and chat among themselves. Yeshua's friends have been gone for hours. Then a chief priest notices Yeshua has not moved for awhile. He walks over to where the soldiers are engrossed in a game and asks the soldier in charge of the crucifixion detail to check on him.

"And if he's not dead, could you, uh, speed up the process?" he asks politely.

"Why should we?"

"Because the Sabbath will begin in three hours and we can't work on the Sabbath. If he dies after six o'clock, or even close to that time, we could not remove the body until Sunday. It would have to remain here all day Saturday."

"So?"

"Well, that can't be allowed. Our Law stipulates that, for reasons of health and sanitation, people's remains must be buried the same day they die. Also, the *Mishnah* — that's our scribal law — states that 'Everyone who allows the dead to remain overnight transgresses a positive command.'"

"I don't care what your laws say," the soldier scoffs, not wanting to quit his game. "Your laws don't obligate us. We're following Rome's standard procedure for executions that's in effect everywhere in the world. It says we're to leave the prisoner on the cross as long as it takes for him to die — an hour, a week, whatever. Then we're to leave the body up there for awhile — a few days at least, but we can leave them up there for weeks if we want to. We let the wild animals have 'em. Let people see what'll happen to them if they defy Rome. That's the whole point of a crucifixion. That's why we do it here, near a busy intersection, so as many people as possible will see."

The priest cringes at the soldier's matter-of-fact attitude toward leaving a dead body unburied. *Animal!* he thinks.

"I'm aware that's what you do everywhere else in the world, but not here. You must be aware that Rome grants an exception for us so that we can bury our dead within the prescribed twenty-four hours of death."

"Yes, of course," the soldier laughs again. "But that assumes the prisoner is dead. We don't bury living people, and your king may still be alive." All the soldiers laugh.

The chief priest ignores the insult and presses his point. "If the prisoner is alive and the Sabbath is approaching, Rome also grants the chief priests the right to ask you to hasten his death. I ask you now to remove the body from the cross if he is dead, and to hasten his death if he is not dead."

The soldier grumbles something unpleasant, but he knows the priest is within his rights, so he ends the game and stands up.

"Let's go," he orders the others, all business now. "Let's do 'em all. Use a spear for the one on the saddle and use the mallet for the other two."

One soldier hoists a heavy wooden mallet to his shoulder and walks to one of the crosses topped by a "thief" placard. Without looking at the man on the cross he swings the mallet back behind his shoulder, then crashes it as hard as he can against the man's shin. The shinbone shatters into a thousand shards and splinters of bone. Ignoring the thief's screams, he repositions himself slightly and shatters his other shinbone the same way. Then the soldier glances up to make certain both legs are useless, and grunts approval when he sees the man's entire weight is hanging from his wrists. Without legs the man can no longer push against the spike through his ankles to relieve the pressure that hanging by his wrists exerts on his lungs. Suffocation, combined with the shock resulting from the shattering of his shinbones, will kill him in a matter of minutes.

The soldier, satisfied with his work, moves on to the second cross marked "thief" and begins to repeat his work.

As he does, the soldier with the spear approaches Yeshua's cross. He will use the spear since breaking Yeshua's legs with the mallet would be useless. The soldiers had used a saddle for Yeshua, so his full weight fell on the post between his legs while his legs dangled uselessly on either side. Therefore, when the saddle was used, the spear was employed to speed deaths on the cross. The soldier looks up at Yeshua and sees he is limp and not breathing.

"This one's already dead," he calls back to his leader.

"Make sure," comes the reply.

Without hesitating, the soldier lifts the spear over his shoulder and rams it through Yeshua's side. There is no response, so the soldier jerks the spear back out. There still is no response.

"Yeah, he's dead," the soldier calls.

He and another soldier lower the cross, rip Yeshua's arms off the spikes, untie his ankles, and toss the body on the ground.

"He's yours," the soldier calls to the chief priests as he walks away.

A wealthy member of the Sanhedrin who believed in Yeshua enough to stand against the mob at his trial, Joseph of Arimathaea, takes control of the body. He moves it a few yards south into a quiet garden where he has cut a cave out of rock to be used for his own tomb. While temple leaders and Roman soldiers watch closely, he anoints Yeshua's body with burial oils. He needs to do more than that, but the Sabbath is rapdly approaching and there is no time. He will return tomorrow and finish. He covers Yeshua's body with a white shroud and sadly walks away. Several men seal the tomb by rolling boulder against its only opening.

Sanhedrin officials want to make certain no one steals the body during the night and claims later that Yeshua's body has been resurrected, so both they and the Roman civil authorities post all-night sentinels around the cave.

The Sanhedrin members, their work complete, begin filing back to their homes in Jerusalem so they will be ready for the Sabbath. They rest easily in the knowledge that Yeshua is dead, and never again will be a problem for anyone.

Afterword

When Jesus of Nazareth died under circumstances very similar to those described for Yeshua, his disciples all despaired. Fear, disillusionment, disappointment, and confusion overwhelmed them. They had put their faith and hope in Jesus, even believed him to be the Messiah. But now he was dead, and a dead Messiah was no Messiah at all.

The disciples cowered together behind locked doors in Jerusalem. They planned to hide there during the Sabbath, then escape the city Sunday morning by melting into the huge throng of Passover celebrants.

However, when Sunday afternoon arrived, the disciples, instead of scurrying to safety as they had planned, were joyfully proclaiming in the streets and in the temple that Jesus of Nazareth was alive! He had defeated the grave, overcome death, and risen from the grave!

They proclaimed it in the face of the Sanhedrin members who had just had Jesus crucified, and who had the power and the will to have them crucified as well. When the temple leaders threatened them with immediate crucifixion if they didn't stop preaching their nonsense, the disciples proclaimed it even more joyously. Nothing would silence them. They had seen him, touched him, and talked with him! He was alive!

203

What happened on that Sunday morning that caused such an astounding — and permanent — turnaround?

An exact accounting may never be known because the primary sources of information — the books of Matthew, Mark, Luke, John, and the writings of Paul — all tell different stories.

They relate different versions of who went to Jesus' tomb early Sunday morning and found it empty. They disagree as to who met them at the tomb and what was said there. They tell contradictory stories of when and where the resurrected Jesus appeared, and what he said when he appeared.

The first written mention of Jesus' resurrection came in a letter Paul wrote to the fledgling church at Corinth, Greece, two decades after Jesus' death. Although the letter does not mention the empty tomb, it does name six appearances of the risen Jesus: first to Peter, then to the disciples, then to 500 people, then to the apostle James, then to all the apostles, and lastly to Paul himself as he walked along the road from Jerusalem to Damascus. Paul provides no details of any of the sightings, although two sightings (Jesus' appearances to the 500 people and to the apostle James) are not mentioned anywhere else in the Bible.

The book of Matthew, written shortly after the destruction of Jerusalem in 70 A.D., or about thirty-five years after Jesus' death, reports on two appearances of the risen Jesus: first to the women who went to the tomb, then some time later to the eleven disciples on a mountain in Galilee.

Luke, writing about the same time as Matthew, records three appearances, all on the first Sunday: first to two believers as they walked along the road from Jerusalem toward Emmaus, then to Peter alone, and finally to all the disciples in Jerusalem.

John, writing in 85 A.D. or later, relates four appearances: first to Mary Magdalene Sunday morning, then to ten of the disciples (everyone but Thomas) behind closed doors later that day; then to all of the disciples (including Thomas) a week later; and finally to seven disciples some time after that as they fished on the Sea of Galilee. John also says Peter and a disciple he did not name, but apparently was John himself, ran to the tomb after Mary told them Yeshua had risen from the grave and confirmed for themselves that the tomb was empty.

Mark, who wrote around 65 A.D., does not mention any appearances of the risen Jesus. However, most scholars agree the original ending of Mark has been lost, and the lost pages almost certainly contained reports of sightings. They point out that Mark predicted a post-death appearance five times, and the pages immediately preceding the lost pages described how the women found the tomb empty and how a "young man" met them at the tomb and told them Jesus had risen.

But even though the sources disagree on many details, all five agree emphatically and unshakably on the one essential point that Jesus rose from the dead and was alive. To them the resurrection was not a philosophical argument, not a matter of faith, not a hallucination. It was an established fact, an event they witnessed, and they would proclaim it for the rest of their lives even though they knew they could be, and probably would be, tortured and killed for doing so. They had absolutely nothing to gain and everything to lose, and yet they would not be silenced.

But did Jesus actually, literally, rise bodily from the dead?

There is, of course, no proof that he did or did not, so ultimately the story must be accepted or rejected on faith alone. However, there is strong evidence to support both sides of the question.

Naysayers maintain that the resurrection story raises at least two questions that cannot be answered without contradicting the whole resurrection story: What was the nature of the resurrected body? And what happened to the physical body?

1. What was the nature of the resurrected body? If the resurrected body was a physical body, it would explain how Jesus could eat with his disciples and invite them to touch him, but it would raise questions of how he could appear in closed and locked rooms or walk seven miles with two followers without their recognizing him. However, if the resurrected body was a spiritual body, the reverse would be true. It would explain how Jesus could get into closed and locked rooms and it would account for how he could walk with admirers and not be recognized, but it would raise questions of how he could eat with his disciples and invite them to touch him.

One theory often proffered to explain the dichotomy is that all the people who reported seeing the risen Jesus only had visions. But there are at least three problems with that theory. One, it does not coincide with any of the documentary evidence, all of which insists without apology that the resurrection was real. Two, visions are rarely experienced by more than one person, yet Matthew, Luke, and John name at least sixteen people who saw him; and Paul, who became a believer more than a year after Jesus died, sets the number at more than 500 — most of whom he said were still alive as he wrote. And three, people who have visions are almost always feverish with expectation before their visions occur, but in Jerusalem that morning, the opposite conditions existed. The disciples and their friends were feeling sorrow, disappointment, abandonment, dejection, confusion, and fear — hardly the conditions for a vision, and certainly not a vision that would affect between sixteen and 500 people, in different times and in different places.

2. What happened to Jesus' physical body? Although this question has never been answered to the satisfaction or agreement of all people who call themselves Christians, many have attempted to answer. Among the theories:

— *Someone, probably the disciples, bribed the tomb's guards and took the body so they could claim Jesus had been resurrected.* This is the explanation the New Testament says the Sanhedrin ordered the guards to tell. However, no evidence supports that version. No body was ever produced, and no guard or soldier was ever charged with accepting a bribe or allowing the body to be moved.

— *The physical body ascended into heaven.* This is the view shared by many fundamentalists and other conservative Christians, although it is hard to correlate it with today's understanding of the universe.

— *The physical body was transmuted into a spiritual body.* The scientific basis for this theory is that matter can be converted into energy, and some forms of energy can penetrate rock. There is no evidence, however, that any of the conditions necessary for such a transmutation were present in the tomb with Jesus.

— *The disciples stole the body.* Possible, but unlikely because Jewish guards and Roman soldiers were stationed at the tomb to specifically prevent that. Also, no evidence exists to support the theory.

— *Jesus' body was buried with the thieves' at a common burial ground.* Maybe, but it runs counter to all the documentary evidence that says he was buried in a garden tomb that belonged to a friend.

— *The Romans or Jews disposed of the body.* Very unlikely. If they had the body, they would have produced it to stop the talk that Jesus had been resurrected.

— *Mary and the other women went to the wrong tomb.* Again, very unlikely. At the very least, four people went to the tomb, and it's hard to believe all of them made the same mistake.

— *We don't know, and it doesn't matter.* Many non-fundamentalist Christians contend that although they do not know the answers to all the questions that grow out of the resurrection story, the issue ultimately is not important. They point out that Jesus never made belief in his Messiahship or the resurrection a condition of discipleship. Rather, Jesus insisted only that his followers love God and love one another. That, and nothing more.

However, despite the unanswered, and perhaps unanswerable, questions, a solid body of evidence exists that supports the story of the resurrection.

The writings of Matthew, Mark, Luke, John, and Paul, already detailed, speak for themselves — especially when it's realized that the writers were honorable, trustworthy men who had nothing to gain and everything to lose by writing.

But there is other evidence, most of it circumstantial, that also supports the resurrection story. Circumstantial evidence alone proves nothing, but it does add great weight to the documentary evidence. Examples:

— *The early actions of the disciples.* Aside from a resurrection, how can the disciples' actions possibly be explained? One moment they are fleeing in despair, fear, disillusionment, and confusion; the next moment they are joyously risking their lives to proclaim Jesus had risen from the dead.

They knew they could and probably would die horrible deaths for what they were doing. Yet, even when they were threatened with the cross, they refused to recant or be silent. They proclaimed all the more. Clearly, something overwhelming happened that Sunday morning at Jerusalem. And all the people involved insist — adamantly, fearlessly, consistently, and joyfully — that what happened was the resurrection of Jesus. If the story were not true, why would they invite horrible, agonizing crucifixions to proclaim it? (Note: According to legend, or "remembered fact," all the disciples except John died violent deaths because of their teaching. And when Peter was told he was to be nailed to a cross, he begged to be nailed upside down because he was not worthy to die as his master had. His wish apparently was granted. As for John, he lived many years, and in late life he was the mind, if not the hand, behind the book of John, which is generally considered to be one of the greatest masterpieces of religious literature ever written.)

— *The existence of the New Testament.* The authors of every one of the New Testament's twenty-seven books were convinced beyond any shred of doubt that Jesus' resurrection was a reality and that he was alive and working when they wrote. Why would they risk their lives and reputations to write glorious lies about a man who died either a madman or a liar, or both, but certainly an abject failure? The fact that the writings were later elevated to the status of canonized Scripture attests further to their validity.

— *The existence of the Christian church.* From the very beginning, Christians organized the church to commune with a living savior, not to memorialize a dead failure. In the ensuing 2,000 years, that mission has never changed. How can the church's birth, growth, and continued existence for 2,000 years be accounted for apart from the resurrection?

— *The observance of Sunday as the Christian day of worship.* The Ten Commandments, one of Judaism's most important foundation documents, specifically mandates that the Sabbath (Saturday, the seventh day) be kept holy. From earliest history down to this day, Jews have held that commandment to be inviolable. However, even though virtually all early Christians were loyal Jews, they quickly changed their primary day of worship to Sunday because they were absolutely certain that Jesus rose from the dead on Sunday. Apart from the resurrection, there is no way to explain why so many religious Jews would so willingly, even eagerly, abandon one of their sacrosanct Ten Commandments.

— *The joyous celebration of the Eucharist.* The Eucharist (also known as Communion and the Lord's Supper) is a church service that commemorates the death of Jesus, yet it contains no hint of mourning. It is a joyful service — the word Eucharist means thanksgiving. Neither the service's joyful nature nor its continued celebration for two thousand years can be easily explained had Jesus not risen from the dead.

— *The Bible's appeal to one's sense of truth.* For many Christians, proof that the Bible is true is that it kindles those who speak its word to high and great expression, and those who hear it to respond to its greatness. The Gospel stories in general, and the resurrection story in particular, are the basis for much of the world's greatest music, literature, painting, sculpture, drama and all other expressions of art. They have encouraged and fortified countless people to commit acts of heroism, large and small, over two millenniums, and they still do. It appeals to our sense of truth and, therefore, proves itself to us.

— *Experiential evidence*. For most Christians, by far the most compelling evidence that Jesus overcame death is that he is still alive, and anyone who wants to experience him can do so simply by living his commandments and observing the results. If living Jesus' commandments (loving God and loving one another) produces the results he promised (joy, fearlessness, and trouble), it is evidence Jesus still lives. And if living his commandments does not produce the results he promised, it is evidence he was a liar, a madman, or both.

Still, it is unfair to expect anyone to believe in the resurrection if that person has not experienced the living Jesus, just as it is unfair for anyone to deny the resurrection if he has not put himself in a position where he can experience it. Without experience, everything else is mere opinion.

Nevertheless, regardless of whether Jesus rose from the dead, is he the Messiah?

The term is an ancient Jewish word used to describe an ancient Jewish concept, and all three major divisions of Judaism — Orthodox, Conservative, and Reform — insist that Jesus is not their Messiah. Christians, on the other hand, contend Jesus is the Messiah and the Jews simply did not recognize him when he came.

Whether Jesus did or did not rise bodily from the grave, or is or is not the Messiah, something remarkable undoubtedly happened on that Sunday morning in Jerusalem that elevated an itinerant spiritual teacher to the most powerful force the world has ever known.

So could Jesus have been divine in some other way, other than being the Messiah?

That question raises the most intriguing question of all: If you look at Jesus and see God, what's the difference?

Acknowledgments

No book is solely the product of one person. I would like to acknowledge my gratitude to some of the people who have helped make this book a reality.

Herald Latham, Dew James, and Jimmy Howle, former editors with *The Florence* [S.C] *Morning News,* and Stanley Atkins and Rex N. Thomas, former correspondents with The Associated Press, who took the time and made the effort to impress upon a cub reporter the strength and beauty of simplicity.

Dr. Barbara Derrick, a United Methodist minister, counselor, editor, and writer, who was friend enough to tell me the painful truth about an early version of this book.

Dr. Richard Johnson, a teacher of religion at Charleston Southern University, and Rabbi William A. Rosenthall, who graciously gave of their time and knowledge to guide my accuracy while I reduced thousands of years of intricate Jewish history to a few typewritten pages.

Dr. Elizabeth Burnett, a historian of Christian theology and this book's primary editor, who has been a godsend from the first time our paths crossed.

Dr. Pinhas Porat, Holy Land archeologist, former director of antiquities for the Galilee area, and acting director of Bethsaida excavations; and Nova Cohen, biblical archeologist attached to the Hebrew University of Jerusalem, who so willingly shared their wealth of knowledge about the Holy Land, past and present.

Jimmy Nammour, Christian-Palestinian native of Jerusalem and a Holy Land guide with Educational Opportunities, Inc., who led me along the paths Jesus walked 2,000 years ago.

Dr. A. C. Holler, United Methodist minister and counselor, who, along with Barbara Derrick, taught me the techniques and showed me the values of meditating.

Richard N. Côté, author, editor, and publisher of Corinthian Books, whose encouragement and faith in my writing has been unending; and his copy editors Sarah Williams and Sandra White, who walked the extra mile without being asked to make this book as good as they could make it.

However, the views and conclusions presented here are solely my own and do not necessarily represent the opinions of my many respected advisers.